Comptroller of the Currency
Administrator of National Banks

I0439078

Related Organizations

Comptroller's Handbook

August 2004

Management

Related Organizations

Corporate Governance

Table of Contents

Introduction

This booklet is designed as a reference tool and examination guide to assist bankers and examiners in understanding the various types of related organizations, risks that may be associated with these organizations, and the responsibilities of a bank's board of directors and management to institute strong and effective corporate practices governing the bank's relationships with these organizations.

As used in this booklet, the term "related organizations" refers to various types of entities related to a national bank, typically by common ownership or control, including certain advisory relationships. Generally, related organizations are affiliates or subsidiaries, each with its own legal definition. Related organizations can include bank holding companies, operating subsidiaries, financial subsidiaries, statutory subsidiaries, chain banking organizations, community development corporations, and related interests of principal shareholders.

The OCC's supervision by risk approach takes into account current and planned activities of all related entities, including nonbank subsidiaries and affiliates, to determine how much risk they pose to the bank. Studies have shown that inappropriate relationships with related organizations, including insider abuse, rank high on the list of causes of bank problems. Improperly managed relationships with related organizations have been a factor in numerous bank failures.

Related organizations have become increasingly important to banks in recent years as the scope of activities they conduct has expanded and their geographic locations have multiplied. The passage of the Gramm–Leach–Bliley Act of 1999 (GLBA) removed some of the previous barriers between banking and other financial activities and services. For example, now a "financial subsidiary" of a national bank may conduct certain activities that are not otherwise authorized for the bank itself, such as underwriting securities of all types, provided that the activities are financial in nature or incidental to a financial activity. The new opportunities for transactions with related organizations may introduce new risks that need to be understood and properly managed.

Related organizations can provide opportunities for product diversification, augmentation of the customer base, geographic expansion or joint investment, and increased consolidated earnings. Conversely, a bank's relationship with a related organization can create conflicts of interest and present complex corporate governance and risk management issues. These issues, if not properly addressed, can lead to a reduction in the bank's or parent company's income stream or capital.

Sections 23A and 23B of the Federal Reserve Act (12 USC 371c and 371c-1), as implemented by Regulation W (12 CFR 223), contain quantitative and qualitative restrictions on a bank's transactions with its affiliates. While these provisions primarily protect a bank from suffering credit losses on loans to affiliates, a bank's relationship with its affiliates also may introduce other material risks, including reputation and strategic risks. The board and management must remain aware of and appropriately manage these types of risk.

GLBA also codified the concept of "functional regulation," establishing a regulatory framework for certain activities conducted within banks and through functionally regulated subsidiaries and affiliates. While GLBA altered the Office of the Comptroller of the Currency's direct responsibility over functionally regulated entities and activities, the Office of the Comptroller of the Currency (OCC) maintains a vital interest in and responsibilities for understanding all risks affecting national banks, including those posed by related organizations that are functionally regulated by other regulators. A discussion of the functional regulation framework is in this booklet's "Supervision of Related Organizations" section.

An effective and sound corporate governance structure must include policies and procedures identifying board and management expectations, roles, and responsibilities pertaining to related organizations. The board and management are responsible for ensuring that all dealings between the bank and its related organizations serve the bank's best interests and are appropriately monitored and controlled. Such relationships should be subject to robust corporate governance practices and risk management policies. No matter what the legal relationship is between a bank and its related organizations, a prudent financial and managerial relationship must exist. The bank's board of directors should adopt appropriate policies and procedures to ensure that the bank's relationship with its affiliates and other related organizations is sound and appropriately documented. Also, the board should appropriately monitor and manage any conflicts of interest that arise between related organizations and any of the bank's directors, members of management, and principal shareholders.

Types of Related Organizations

This section briefly describes the various related organizations covered by this booklet. These related organizations include affiliates; operating, financial, and statutory subsidiaries; bank holding companies; chain banking organizations; parallel-owned banking organizations; foreign branches and subsidiaries; community development corporations; noncontrolling equity investments; and companies owned or controlled by principal shareholders.

Related organizations are organized under and subject to various laws and regulations. Regardless of the legal structure of a bank's related organizations, an essential element of the bank's safe and sound operation is the properly documented and well-supervised relationship between the bank and these organizations.

The following chart reflects the laws and regulations commonly applicable to a bank's investment in and transactions with its subsidiaries and affiliates:

Law or Regulation	General Purpose[1]
12 USC 24(Seventh)	Authorizes and limits a bank's investment in subsidiaries other than financial subsidiaries.
12 USC 24(Eleventh)	Authorizes and limits a bank's public welfare investments, including purchasing equity interests in entities engaged in making investments designed primarily to promote the public welfare.
12 USC 24a	Authorizes a bank to conduct in financial subsidiaries certain activities that are financial in nature but not otherwise authorized for the bank itself.
12 USC 221a	Defines "affiliate" except where otherwise specifically provided.
Section 23A of the Federal Reserve Act (12 USC 371c)	Defines "affiliate" for purposes of restrictions on transactions with affiliates. Restricts the amount of a bank's "covered" transactions with its affiliates and requires collateral that secures certain transactions to meet quantitative and qualitative standards. Requires all transactions with affiliates to be consistent with safe and sound banking practices.
Section 23B of the Federal Reserve Act (12 USC 371c-1)	Requires a bank's transactions with its affiliates to be at arm's length.
Regulation W (12 CFR 223)	Implements sections 23A and 23B, incorporating new GLBA requirements with years of guidelines and interpretations issued by the Federal Reserve Board into one rule.
12 CFR 5.34–5.39	Sets forth authorized activities and notice or application procedures for banks engaging in activities through certain subsidiaries and noncontrolling investments.
12 CFR 24	Implements 12 USC 24(Eleventh) and sets forth notice and application procedures for banks engaging in public welfare investments.

---

[1] This chart describes only the general purposes of the cited laws and regulations. To understand the laws and regulations fully, please review them closely.

Affiliates

Generally, an "affiliate" is an entity that controls a bank, that is controlled by a bank, or that is under common control with a bank. While there is no all-purpose definition of affiliate, the definition in 12 USC 221a is generally used in contexts other than the legal restrictions that apply to a bank's transactions with its affiliates. Under 12 USC 221a, the term "affiliate" includes any corporation, business trust, association, or other similar organization in which:

- The bank, directly or indirectly, owns or controls either a majority of the voting shares or more than 50 percent of the shares voted in the preceding election of directors, trustees, or other persons exercising similar functions;

- The bank controls in any manner the election of a majority of the directors, trustees, or other persons exercising similar functions;

- Control is held, directly or indirectly, through stock ownership or in any other manner, by the shareholders of the bank who own or control either a majority of the shares of such bank or more than 50 percent of the shares voted in its preceding election of directors or by trustees for the benefit of the shareholders of any such bank;

- The directors of a single bank form a majority of the organization's directors, trustees, or other persons exercising similar functions;

- The organization owns or controls, directly or indirectly, either a majority of the shares of capital stock of a bank or more than 50 percent of the shares voted in the preceding election of directors of a bank;

- The organization controls, in any manner, the election of a majority of the directors of a bank; or

- The organization's trustees hold all, or substantially all, of a bank's capital stock for the benefit of the organization's shareholders or members.

Sections 23A and 23B of the Federal Reserve Act, and their implementing regulation, Regulation W, contain a slightly different definition of the term "affiliate" than 12 USC 221a. This definition, described later in this booklet in the section entitled "Transactions with Affiliates," is used for purposes of applying legal restrictions on a bank's transactions with its affiliates.

Subsidiaries

Structure

A bank may conduct its activities or deliver its products or services to customers by means of subsidiaries. The controlling interest that the bank owns in a subsidiary can be in the form of voting stock in a corporation or equivalent interests in other entities, such as partnerships or limited liability companies.

Corporation

A bank may own a subsidiary that is organized as a corporation under state law or, in some cases, federal law. In such circumstances, the bank owns stock of the subsidiary corporation. Owning shares of stock gives the right to share proportionally in the profits of the corporation and in the distribution of assets upon dissolution, after payment of debt. Normally, shareholders are protected from liability for the debts and obligations of the corporation.

Limited Liability Company

A limited liability company (LLC) is an unincorporated business organization established under state law that limits the liability of its members while allowing them to participate actively in the entity's management. Although members generally are protected from liability to the same extent as shareholders of a corporation, the LLC has a certain advantage over a corporation; that is, it may be treated as a partnership for federal tax purposes. The LLC is not a taxable entity and its earnings flow through untaxed to the members.

Partnership

A bank also can own interests in partnerships established under state law that engage in bank permissible activities. State laws generally define a partnership as an association of two or more persons to carry on as co-owners of a business for profit. Because general partners assume unlimited liability for the acts of other partners within the scope of the partnership, national banks may not serve as general partners. A national bank may, however, set up an operating subsidiary to enter into a general partnership. Because the operating subsidiary, and not the bank, will be the partner, the bank's potential liability should be contained.

A national bank may be a limited partner in a partnership engaged in permissible activities. A limited partner's liability is limited to the amount of its investment in the limited partnership. For this reason, a national bank may participate in a limited partnership directly, although an operating subsidiary also may be used. A national bank must not exercise management control as a limited partner because doing so could cause it to lose its limited liability and be treated as a general partner.

Whenever a national bank participates in a partnership, either directly or through an operating subsidiary, it must be able to ensure that the partnership's activities are permissible for national banks either by controlling the conduct of the business or by possessing the power to veto impermissible activities. If the national bank does not possess either of these powers, it must have the power to withdraw (and it must indeed withdraw) from a partnership that performs or is about to perform impermissible activities.

Types of Subsidiaries

For OCC purposes, there are three types of bank subsidiaries: operating subsidiaries, financial subsidiaries, and statutory subsidiaries.

Operating Subsidiaries

An operating subsidiary is a corporation, LLC, or similar entity that engages in activities that are part of, or incidental to, the business of banking as determined by the OCC or other statutory authority. The bank must either (1) own more than 50 percent of the voting or similar type of controlling interest, or (2) otherwise control the subsidiary when no party controls more than 50 percent (or a percentage greater than the bank's interest) of the voting or similar type of controlling interest.

Operating subsidiaries are governed by 12 CFR 5.34. This section does not apply to (1) financial subsidiaries and statutory subsidiaries (both discussed immediately below) and (2) any subsidiaries in which the bank has acquired, in good faith, shares through foreclosure on collateral, by way of compromise of a doubtful claim, or to avoid a loss in connection with a debt previously contracted.

Types of Activities and Filing Qualifications

A bank that intends to acquire or establish an operating subsidiary, perform a new activity in an existing operating subsidiary, or make a new noncontrolling investment through an operating subsidiary, usually must submit an application or notice to the OCC. The bank's condition and the subsidiary's activity determine the way a bank files with the OCC.

Operating subsidiary filings may take one of two forms: an after-the-fact notice or a standard application. Only well-capitalized and well-managed banks may file under the notice process for "eligible activities." If a bank does not qualify or if the activities proposed are not eligible for the after-the-fact notice process, the bank must follow the standard application process. (See the *Comptroller's Licensing Manual* for detailed guidance on operating subsidiary filing procedures.)

After-the-Fact Notice

The after-the-fact notice category contains commonly accepted banking-related activities that the OCC has previously approved for subsidiaries. Under this process, a well-capitalized and well-managed bank may file an after-the-fact notice for specific activities as listed in the "activities eligible for notice" section (12 CFR 5.34(e)(5)(v)) in the regulation. Under this process, a bank files a written notice with the OCC within 10 days after establishing or acquiring the subsidiary, or commencing the activity, and need not seek prior OCC approval.

To qualify for the notice process, the bank that wishes to establish or acquire the subsidiary must be "well managed" as set forth in 12 CFR 5.34(d)(3) and "well capitalized" as defined at 12 CFR 6.4(b):

- Unless otherwise determined in writing by the OCC, to be "well managed" a national bank must have a composite rating of 1 or 2 under the Uniform Financial Institutions Rating System or an equivalent system on its most recent examination. If the institution has not been examined, then it must have managerial resources that the OCC determines are satisfactory.

- "Well capitalized" means that the capital level is designated as "well capitalized" pursuant to 12 CFR 6.4(b) (Prompt Corrective Action).[2]

Any bank receiving approval pursuant to the notice process is deemed to have represented that the subsidiary will conduct the activity in a manner consistent with the OCC's guidance and under the same terms and conditions as would apply if the activity were conducted directly by the bank.

The activities qualifying for the after-the-fact notice process are listed in appendix A of this booklet.

Operating Subsidiary Application

A proposal to acquire or establish an operating subsidiary or to perform new activities in an existing subsidiary must undergo the OCC's standard application review process when the proposed activities do not qualify for after-the-fact notice, when the bank will control and own 50 percent or less of the interest in an operating subsidiary, or when the bank is not "well capitalized" and "well managed" as defined by the regulation.

The OCC may require the applicant to submit a legal analysis if the proposal is novel, is unusually complex, or raises substantial unresolved legal issues. In such cases, the OCC encourages applicants to arrange a pre-filing meeting with the OCC. Additionally, any bank subject to supervisory concerns should provide financial information to support the proposed transaction (e.g., strategic plan, cost projections, or pro forma financial projections).

---

[2] With respect to operating subsidiaries, financial subsidiaries, and noncontrolling equity investments, the term "well capitalized" means the bank (1) has a total risk-based capital ratio of 10.0 percent or greater, (2) has a Tier 1 risk-based capital ratio of 6.0 percent or greater, (3) has a leverage ratio of 5.0 percent or greater, and (4) is not subject to any written agreement, order, capital directive, or prompt corrective action directive issued by the OCC to meet and maintain a specific capital level for any capital measure.

Any bank filing under the standard application review process must receive an approval decision before acquiring or establishing the operating subsidiary or commencing the new activity.

Financial Subsidiaries

A financial subsidiary is any company that is controlled by one or more insured depository institutions, other than a subsidiary that is an operating subsidiary or statutory subsidiary, that engages in activities that are financial in nature or incidental to a financial activity. A financial subsidiary does not engage *solely* in activities in which a national bank may engage directly. However, a financial subsidiary may *combine* financial activities that are otherwise impermissible for the bank to conduct directly and that are defined in the GLBA, or determined to be financial in nature or incidental to a financial activity by the Secretary of the Treasury (in consultation with the Board of Governors of the Federal Reserve System), with activities in which national banks are permitted to engage directly. Financial subsidiaries are governed by 12 USC 24a (enacted in GLBA) and 12 CFR 5.39.

Types of Financial Activities

Financial subsidiaries may engage in:

- Lending, exchanging, transferring, investing for others, or safeguarding money or securities.

- Activities as agent or broker in any state for purposes of insuring, guaranteeing, or indemnifying against loss, harm, damage, illness, disability, death, or defects in title (under certain conditions); or providing annuities as agent or broker.

- Providing financial, investment, or economic advisory services, including advising an investment company as defined in section 3 of the Investment Company Act (15 USC 880a–3).

- Issuing or selling instruments representing interests in pools of assets permissible for a bank to hold directly.

- Underwriting, dealing in, or making a market in securities.

- Any activity that the Board of Governors of the Federal Reserve System has determined, by order or regulation in effect on November 12,

1999, to be a proper incident of banking (subject to the same terms and conditions contained in the order or regulation, unless the order or regulation is modified by the Board of Governors of the Federal Reserve System).

- Any activity, in the United States, that a bank holding company may engage in outside the United States and that the Board of Governors of the Federal Reserve System has determined, under regulations prescribed or interpretations issued pursuant to section 4(c)(13) of the Bank Holding Company Act of 1956 (12 USC 1843(c)(13)) as in effect on November 11, 1999, to be usual in connection with the transaction of banking or other financial operations abroad.

- Other activities that the Secretary of the Treasury, in consultation with the Board of Governors of the Federal Reserve System, as provided in 12 USC 24a, determines to be financial in nature or incidental to a financial activity.

- As provided by regulations issued by Secretary of the Treasury pursuant to 12 USC 24a:

  - Lending, exchanging, transferring, investing for others, or safeguarding financial assets other than money or securities;

  - Providing any device or other instrumentality for transferring money or other financial assets; and

  - Arranging, effecting, or facilitating financial transactions for the account of third parties.

Financial subsidiaries of a national bank are generally prohibited from engaging as principal in insurance underwriting (except for "authorized products," as defined in the GLBA, and certain other insurance products as provided by the GLBA), real estate investment and development, or merchant banking activities that are permitted under paragraph (H) or (I) of section 4(k)(4) of the Bank Holding Company Act of 1956 (12 USC 1843(k)(4)(H) and (I)) unless the Board of Governors of the Federal Reserve System and the Secretary of the Treasury adopt joint regulations after November 12, 2004, that allow financial subsidiaries to engage in merchant banking activities under subparagraph H.

Filing Qualifications

A bank that intends to acquire control of, or hold an interest in, a financial subsidiary, or to commence a new activity in an existing financial subsidiary, must obtain OCC approval through certification and notice procedures. Because GLBA requires OCC approval to be based only on specific statutory factors, the OCC considers a filing to be approved upon receipt of the bank's submission of the notice and appropriate certification that it meets the statutory criteria.

Pursuant to 12 CFR 5.39, there are two options for filing a notice. Under the first option, the bank files a "Financial Subsidiary Certification" at any time and files a notice at the time it acquires control of or holds an interest in a financial subsidiary, or commences a new activity in an existing financial subsidiary. Under the second method, the bank files a combined certification and notice five business days before it acquires control of, or holds an interest in, a financial subsidiary, or commences a new activity in an existing financial subsidiary

Only qualifying banks are permitted to file. To meet the qualifying bank requirement, a national bank and each of its depository institution affiliates must meet certain criteria to control or hold an interest in a financial subsidiary. These criteria are as follows:

- The national bank and each of its depository institution affiliates must:

  - Be "well managed." That is, unless otherwise determined in writing by the appropriate federal banking agency, it must have a composite rating of 1 or 2, *as well as a rating of 1 or 2 on the management element*, under the Uniform Financial Institutions Rating System or an equivalent system. If the institution has not been examined, then it must have managerial resources that the OCC determines are satisfactory; and

  - Be "well capitalized." That is, its capital level must satisfy the definition of "well capitalized" in 12 CFR 6, Prompt Corrective Action.

- The aggregate consolidated total assets of all financial subsidiaries of the national bank must not exceed the lesser of 45 percent of the consolidated total assets of the parent bank or $50 billion. (The $50 billion limit is subject to adjustment according to an indexing mechanism established jointly by the Secretary of the Treasury and the Federal Reserve Board (FRB).)

- A national bank that is one of the 100 largest insured banks, determined on the basis of the bank's consolidated total assets at the end of the calendar year, must have outstanding eligible long-term debt that is currently rated in one of the three highest investment-grade rating categories by a nationally recognized statistical rating organization. If a national bank is one of the second 50 of the 100 largest insured banks, the bank may satisfy the eligible debt requirement either by meeting the standard above or by receiving a qualifying long-term issuer credit rating from at least one nationally recognized statistical rating organization. The rating must be one of the three highest investment grade ratings issued by the organization, and it must be current. A long-term issuer credit rating is a written opinion, issued by a nationally recognized statistical rating organization, of the bank's overall capacity and willingness to pay on a timely basis its unsecured, dollar-denominated financial obligations maturing in not less than one year. If the financial subsidiary is engaging solely in activities in an agency capacity, the eligible debt requirement does not apply.

Community Reinvestment Act (CRA) Requirements

A national bank cannot commence a new financial activity in a financial subsidiary or acquire control of a financial subsidiary if the bank or any of its insured depository institution affiliates received a less than "satisfactory" CRA rating on its most recent CRA exam prior to the bank's filing of its notice. National banks that have not yet received a CRA rating and special purpose banks which are not CRA-rated may submit a notice if they meet all of the other qualifications and safeguards.

Safety and Soundness Safeguards

GLBA and 12 CFR 5.39 require a national bank to meet certain safeguards when engaging in activities through a financial subsidiary:

- For purposes of determining regulatory capital:

  - The bank must deduct the aggregate amount of its outstanding equity investment, including retained earnings, in its financial subsidiaries from its total assets and tangible equity, and deduct such investment from its total risk-based capital (this deduction shall be made equally from Tier 1 and Tier 2 capital); and

  - The bank may not consolidate the assets and liabilities of a financial subsidiary with those of the bank.

- Any published financial statement of the bank shall, in addition to providing information prepared in accordance with generally accepted accounting principles, separately present financial information for the bank in the manner provided above.

- The bank must have reasonable policies and procedures to maintain the separate corporate identity and limited liability of the national bank and the financial subsidiaries of the bank.

- The bank must have procedures for identifying and managing operational and financial risk within the bank and the financial subsidiary that adequately protect the bank from those risks.

- The bank must treat the financial subsidiary generally as if it were a nonbank affiliate and not a subsidiary of the bank for purposes of the affiliate transaction and the anti-tying rules.

The bank and, as appropriate, any affiliated depository institutions must continue to satisfy the well-capitalized and well-managed requirements and the safeguards described above after acquiring control of, or investing in, a financial subsidiary. Failure to do so could result in limits on the activities of the national bank, its subsidiaries, or an insured depository institution affiliate, or even a requirement to divest control of the financial subsidiary.

Statutory Subsidiaries

A statutory subsidiary is organized under the authority of a specific statute. Although a bank can usually acquire or establish a statutory subsidiary without the OCC's prior approval, certain investments require prior notification. Unless otherwise noted, no prior notification or approval is required to acquire or establish the following types of a statutory subsidiary:

Agricultural Credit Corporation [12 USC 24(Seventh)]

A bank may purchase, for its own account, stock of a corporation organized to make loans to farmers and ranchers for agricultural purposes. Such equity investments in agricultural credit corporations are limited to 20 percent of the unimpaired capital and unimpaired surplus of the bank, unless it owns at least 80 percent of the stock of the agricultural credit corporation. While prior approval is not required, written notice must be provided to the appropriate OCC office within 10 days after making such an investment. (See 12 CFR 5.36 and the *Comptroller's Licensing Manual*, "Investment in Subsidiaries and Equities," for additional information.)

Banker's Bank [12 USC 24(Seventh)]

A banker's bank is a national or state bank engaged exclusively in providing services to or for other depository institutions and holding companies, and their officers, directors, and employees. A banker's bank must be owned exclusively (except for directors' qualifying shares, if any) by insured depository institutions or their holding companies. A bank may invest up to 10 percent of its capital and surplus in an insured banker's bank or in the holding company of such a bank, provided that it does not own more than 5 percent of any class of voting securities.[3]

Safe Deposit Corporation [12 USC 24(Seventh)]

A safe deposit corporation is a corporation that is organized under state law to conduct a safe deposit business. Investment in a safe deposit corporation may not exceed 15 percent of the bank's unimpaired, paid-in capital and 15 percent of its unimpaired surplus.

State Housing Corporation [12 USC 24(Seventh)]

A national bank may make an equity investment in any state housing corporation incorporated in the state in which the bank is located, provided

---

[3] Although OCC approval is not required to make an equity investment in a banker's bank, the banker's bank itself must receive charter approval from the appropriate regulator.

that its investments do not exceed 5 percent of its unimpaired, paid-in capital stock plus 5 percent of its unimpaired surplus fund.

Community and Economic Development Entities [12 USC 24(Eleventh)]

A community and economic development entity (CEDE) is an entity that makes investments or conducts activities that primarily benefit low- and moderate-income individuals, low- and moderate-income areas, or other areas targeted by a governmental entity for redevelopment. An entity that makes qualifying investments under the Community Reinvestment Act (12 CFR 25.23) is also deemed a CEDE. CEDEs are discussed in more detail below.

Bank Premises Corporation [12 USC 371d]

A bank may invest in bank premises directly or through a corporation. Equity investments in bank premises corporations are statutory subsidiaries and require no prior approval unless an investment is over the 12 USC 371d limit.

A bank may make an aggregate investment in bank premises up to 150 percent of its capital and surplus without the OCC's prior approval if its composite CAMELS rating is 1 or 2 and it is well-capitalized as defined in 12 CFR 6 before and after it makes the investment or loan. However, the bank must notify the OCC in writing within 30 days after the investment or loan is made. For other national banks, prior OCC approval is required for investments that exceed the amount of the bank's capital stock. (See 12 CFR 5.37 and the "Investment in Bank Premises" booklet of the *Comptroller's Licensing Manual.*)

Savings Associations [12 USC 1823(k)]

Section 13 of the Federal Deposit Insurance Act, as amended by the Financial Institutions Reform, Recovery, and Enforcement Act of 1989, authorizes a bank to acquire a savings association upon determination that severe financial conditions exist and that such an acquisition would lessen the risk to the insurance fund.

A thrift subject to this provision may be held by a national bank as a subsidiary. The OCC considers such a subsidiary to be a statutory subsidiary.

While prior approval is not required, written notice must be provided to the appropriate OCC office within 10 days after a national bank makes such an investment. (See 12 CFR 5.36 and the "Investment in Subsidiaries and Equities" booklet of the *Comptroller's Licensing Manual.)*

National banks may also hold thrifts as financial subsidiaries, under separate authority, with no financial emergency requirement.

Bank Service Company [12 USC 1862]

A bank service company is a corporation or an LLC organized to provide services authorized by the Bank Service Company Act. If the bank service company is a corporation, one or more insured banks own its capital stock. If it is an LLC, its members are one or more insured banks. All shareholders or members must be located in the same state, unless the FRB approves an exception. A bank may not invest more than 10 percent of its capital and surplus in any single bank service company. The bank's total investment in all bank service companies may not exceed 5 percent of the bank's total assets.

A bank service company may perform any activity that is permissible for all of its shareholder or member banks to perform directly, except that it may not take deposits. (See 12 CFR 5.35 and the *Comptroller's Licensing Manual*, "Investment in Subsidiaries and Equities" for additional information.)

Small Business Investment Company [15 USC 682(b)]

A small business investment company (SBIC) is a venture capital firm licensed and regulated by the Small Business Administration (SBA) that provides debt and equity financing to small businesses.[4] The SBA can provide various types of financial assistance such as guaranteeing the debt portion of the SBIC investments, allowing them to leverage private capital.

A bank is authorized to purchase SBIC stock provided that the aggregate amount of such investments does not exceed 5 percent of the bank's capital and surplus. The bank's receipt and retention of a dividend from an SBIC in

---

[4] The size eligibility requirements for small businesses receiving SBA financial assistance through the SBIC program are prescribed by 13 CFR 121.301.

the form of stock of a corporate borrower of the SBIC is not a purchase of stock within the meaning of 12 USC 24(Seventh). (See 12 CFR 7.1015.)

Noncontrolling Equity Investments

The OCC permits banks to own, either directly or through an operating subsidiary, a noncontrolling interest in an enterprise. The enterprise may be a corporation, limited partnership, LLC, or similar entity. Certain noncontrolling equity investments are governed by 12 CFR 5.36.

12 CFR 5.36 provides an after-the-fact notice procedure for qualifying national banks to make certain types of noncontrolling investments. To meet the qualifying requirements, national banks must be well capitalized and well managed, as those terms are defined for operating subsidiaries. The notice must be filed no later than 10 days after making the investment and must contain the following information:

- A clear description of the activities conducted by the entity in which the bank invests.

- A statement that the entity engages in activities listed in 12 CFR 5.34(e)(5)(v), or alternatively an explanation of how the activities are substantively the same as those described in published OCC precedent for noncontrolling investments, and certification that the activities will be conducted in accordance with the same terms and conditions as stated in the precedent.

- A description of how the bank is able to prevent the enterprise from engaging in activities that do not meet the foregoing standards, or how it is able to withdraw its investment.

- A description of how the investment is convenient or useful to the bank in carrying out the bank's business and not a mere passive investment unrelated to its banking business.

- Certification that the bank's loss exposure will be limited, as a legal and accounting matter, and that the bank will not have open-ended liability for the obligations of the enterprise.

- Certification that the bank will account for its investment under the equity or cost method of accounting.

- Certification that the entity agrees to be subject to OCC supervision and examination (subject to certain limits regarding functionally regulated entities and activities).

When a national bank that is not well capitalized or well managed seeks to make a noncontrolling investment directly or when a national bank wishes to invest in an enterprise that engages in activities that are not eligible for the after-the-fact notice procedure, the OCC determines eligibility case by case.

When owning a minority interest in an enterprise, a bank should participate in the company's affairs to the extent practicable in order to identify and be in a position to control any risks that the company presents to the bank. Information documenting the lines of business and current financial status of all such companies should be maintained in the bank's head office.

In addition, banks may own, either directly or indirectly, a noncontrolling interest in an enterprise pursuant to specific statutory authorization. Examples include community and economic development entities (12 USC 24(Eleventh) and 12 CFR Part 24) and small business investment companies (15 USC 682(b)).

Other Related Organizations

Bank Holding Company

Most, but not all, bank holding companies are regulated by the FRB, pursuant to the Bank Holding Company Act. For those bank holding companies regulated by the FRB (BHC), a BHC is any company that has control over any bank or over any company that is or becomes a BHC (12 USC 1841(a)). In this context, "company" means any corporation, partnership, business trust (or most other kinds of trusts), association, or similar organization. Any company generally has control over a bank or BHC if:

- The company directly, indirectly, or acting through one or more other persons owns, controls, or has power to vote 25 percent or more of any class of voting securities of the bank or company,

- The company controls in any manner the election of a majority of the directors or trustees of the bank or company, or

- The FRB determines, after notice and opportunity for hearing, that the company directly or indirectly exercises a controlling influence over the management or policies of the bank or company.

There are also holding companies that own "non-bank banks" and are not regulated by the FRB. "Non-bank banks" in this context are those limited-purpose banks that are grandfathered by the Competitive Equality Banking Act of 1987, which include certain nationally chartered, FDIC-insured credit card banks.

Transactions between a bank and its parent company and nonbank subsidiaries of the parent company are subject to the restrictions of sections 23A and 23B and Regulation W. The requirements and limits pertinent to transactions with affiliates are discussed in this booklet's "Transactions with Affiliates" section.

Pertinent information regarding a bank's parent company and its nonbank subsidiaries can be found in the reports filed with the Securities and Exchange Commission (SEC), if applicable, and with the FRB in the case of a BHC. For a BHC, reports to the FRB include FR Y-6, the "Annual Report of Bank Holding Companies," which contains information on each subsidiary, information on activities of the parent BHC, and financial statements. Other reports that parent companies may be required to file include:

Report	Title
FR Y−6a*	Report of Changes in Investments or Activities
FR Y−8*	Report of Section 23A Transactions with Affiliates
FR Y−9C*	Consolidated Financial Statements for Bank Holding Companies (parallel to the call report for commercial banks)
FR Y−11I*	Annual Financial Statements of Nonbank Subsidiaries
FR Y−11Q*	Quarterly Financial Statements of Nonbank Subsidiaries
FR Y−20	Financial Statements for a BHC Subsidiary Engaged in Bank-Ineligible Securities Underwriting and Dealing
SEC 10−K	Annual Report
SEC 10−Q	Quarterly Report
SEC 8−K	"Current report," filed after material events or corporate changes have occurred.
*These reports apply only to bank holding companies regulated by the FRB.	

Financial Holding Companies

Section 4(k) of the Bank Holding Company Act, 12 USC 1843(k), authorizes affiliations among banks, securities firms, insurance firms, and other financial companies. It provides for the formation of financial holding companies. A BHC that qualifies as a financial holding company may engage in activities that are financial in nature or incidental to a financial activity. Financial holding companies are authorized by statute to engage in designated financial activities, including insurance underwriting and agency activities, securities underwriting, merchant banking, and insurance company portfolio investment activities. In addition, financial holding companies may engage in those activities that the Board of Governors of the Federal Reserve System determines, in conjunction with the Secretary of the Treasury, to be financial in nature or incidental to a financial activity.

Chain Banking Organizations

In a chain banking organization, two or more independently chartered financial institutions, including at least one national bank, are controlled either directly or indirectly by the same individual, family, or group of individuals closely associated in their business dealings.[5] Control generally exists when the common ownership has the ability, directly or indirectly, to control the vote of 25 percent or more of any class of each institution's voting securities; owns at least 25 percent of the equity capital of each institution; controls in any manner the election of a majority of the directors of each institution; or has the power to exercise a controlling influence over the management or policies of each institution.

Members of a chain banking organization are affiliates of each other for purposes of sections 23A and 23B and Regulation W, the same as if they were owned by the same holding company, as long as they meet one of the applicable tests for affiliation. However, the chain banking organization cannot take advantage of the sister-bank exemption (see discussion in the "Transactions with Affiliates" section) because that exemption requires ownership by a holding company.

---

[5] A registered multibank holding company and its subsidiary banks ordinarily are not considered to be a chain banking group unless the holding company is linked to other banking organizations through common control.

Parallel-Owned Banking Groups

In a parallel-owned banking group, at least one U.S. bank and at least one foreign bank are independently chartered but controlled either directly or indirectly by the same individual, family, or group of individuals who are closely associated in their business dealings or who otherwise act in concert. If a person or group of persons controls 10 percent or more of any class of voting shares of a depository institution, the banking agencies may deem the person or group to control the institution. The presence of certain other characteristics may indicate that a bank or bank holding company located in the United States is part of a parallel-owned banking group:

- An individual or group of individuals acting in concert that controls a foreign bank also controls any class of voting shares of a U.S. depository institution, or persons owning or controlling the shares receive financing from or arranged by the foreign bank, especially if the shares of the U.S. depository institution are collateral for the stock purchase loan.

- The U.S. bank or bank holding company has adopted particular or unique policies or strategies similar to those of the foreign bank, such as common or joint marketing strategies, sharing of customer information, cross-selling of products, or linked Web sites.

- An officer or director of the U.S. bank or bank holding company either (1) serves as an officer or director of a foreign bank or (2) controls a foreign bank or is a member of a group of individuals acting in concert or with common ties that controls a foreign bank.

- The name of the U.S. bank or bank holding company is similar to that of the foreign bank.

For purposes of applying legal restrictions on a bank's transactions with its affiliates within a parallel-owned banking group, the 25 percent control threshold in sections 23A and 23B and Regulation W applies. Like chain banking affiliates, members of a parallel-owned banking group that are affiliates cannot take advantage of the sister-bank exemption because that exemption requires ownership by a holding company.

International Investments and Activities

There are various mechanisms by which national banks can participate in international activities. These forms include foreign branches; foreign bank subsidiaries; Edge Act or Agreement corporations, which may be subsidiaries of banks or bank holding companies; international banking facilities (IBFs); and financial subsidiaries. A bank's objective in having a presence overseas determines, in part, the type of entity to establish. If the objective is to explore a market, a small, specialized office might suffice. If the bank desires to increase its lending activities in a foreign market, it might want a more sophisticated entity that is able to monitor the project risk and country risk. Depending upon the host country's entry requirements, foreign banking activities of a U.S. bank may be conducted through a branch or a banking subsidiary. Other influences on the type of presence are bank strategy, tax considerations, and the international expertise of the bank.

Federal banking law permits foreign branches or foreign subsidiaries, including Edge Act or Agreement corporation subsidiaries of U.S. banks, to engage in activities abroad in which a U.S. bank may engage domestically. Subject to local law, a foreign branch or subsidiary may also engage in certain activities abroad that are not generally permitted for banks in the United States. For national banks, these initial and expanded activities abroad must comply with the OCC's 12 CFR 28, International Banking Activities, and the FRB's Regulation K, 12 CFR 211, including possible pre-establishment licensing requirements. For a foreign branch, the expanded activities must usually be related to the business of banking in the country in which it transacts business. For a foreign subsidiary, such as an Edge Act or Agreement corporation, the expanded activities must be of a banking or financial nature or necessary to carry on banking or financial activities. For international banking activities conducted through financial subsidiaries, the activities must comply with 12 USC 24a and 12 CFR 5.39.

Foreign Branches

It is common for U.S. banking organizations that operate abroad to conduct a sizable amount of their international banking activities through foreign branches. These branches are an integral part of the bank rather than separate entities.

Many banks prefer the foreign branch structure to the foreign subsidiary structure because they have direct control over the operations of a branch. Subsidiary ownership can be complex, especially if local law requires a subsidiary to have some percentage of local ownership and a board of directors. In addition, the branch structure may afford other benefits, e.g., the lending limit is usually based upon the consolidated capital of the parent bank rather than the much lower capital of a subsidiary. However, establishing a subsidiary may have advantages in terms of the parent bank protecting itself from the subsidiary's legal liabilities. This may be an advantage particularly in certain emerging markets where the operating environment can be uncertain.

In addition to general banking powers, branches may make investments that are usual for banks in the local country. Subject to local law, branches may engage in activities that are not permissible for national banks in the United States, such as acting as an insurance agent or broker and providing certain types of guarantees.

Extending credit is a major activity of foreign branches. Typical borrowers tend to be foreign banks and multinational corporations of industrialized countries. Direct financing to foreign governments has become less common for U.S. banks, as most foreign governments can issue debt much less costly in the capital markets. Given this type of clientele, foreign branches in the major financial centers have been increasingly engaged in loan syndications, loan management, leasing, project financing, and other activities geared to the large, complex lending required for major industrial projects and general economic development.

Retail banking, especially deposit taking, has become an integral area of foreign bank business for internationally active U.S. banks, as host countries have liberalized their banking markets and removed most restrictions that once protected local banks. In some markets, foreign banks now are the most dominant players and offer full-scale banking products and services.

Edge Act and Agreement Corporations

A depository institution may organize or acquire a separate subsidiary to engage in international banking activities as an Edge Act corporation, which is licensed under federal law by the FRB, or as an Agreement corporation, which is chartered under state law. Congress authorized such subsidiaries principally to encourage foreign trade. An Edge Act or Agreement corporation may not engage, directly or indirectly, in activities in the United States unless they are incidental to its international activities. Incidental activities are described in the FRB's Regulation K, 12 CFR 211.6.

Under Regulation K, an Edge Act or Agreement corporation's investment in a foreign organization can be either an investment in a subsidiary, an investment in a joint venture, or a portfolio investment. Two factors determine which type of investment it is: (1) the percentage of the foreign organization's voting shares or equity owned or controlled by the corporation and (2) whether the foreign organization engages in permissible types of activities and investments. If the Edge or Agreement corporation owns or controls 50 percent or more of the voting shares or equity in an organization, the organization is considered a subsidiary. Generally, an Edge Act or Agreement corporation may invest only in a subsidiary engaged in banking or financial activities and activities incidental to these activities. If the Edge Act or Agreement corporation owns or controls 20 percent but less than 50 percent of the voting shares or equity of an organization, it has invested in a joint venture. A joint venture may have up to 10 percent of its consolidated assets or consolidated revenues attributable to activities that are not banking or financial. An Edge Act or Agreement corporation may make a portfolio investment by owning or controlling up to 20 percent of the voting shares or equity of an organization that may engage in activities that are not banking or financial. These foreign investments are subject to additional limits in the FRB's Regulation K, which describes permissible activities for these three forms of investments. See 12 CFR 211.9 and 211.10.

Regulation K does not permit a member bank to invest directly in a subsidiary, joint venture, or portfolio investment. Generally, these investments must be made through an Edge Act corporation subsidiary of the bank or through the bank holding company.

The amount of capital and surplus that a member bank may invest in Edge Act and Agreement corporations is limited by 12 USC 618 and Regulation K to 10 percent of capital and surplus or 20 percent with approval of the FRB. The FRB is required to examine Edge Act corporations annually and produce a report of their examination.

As an alternative, a national bank could conduct its international banking activities through a financial subsidiary. In a financial subsidiary, the international activities must comply with 12 USC 24a and 12 CFR 5.39; they are not subject to Regulation K.

Foreign Subsidiaries

In general, a foreign subsidiary is a bank or other company that is separately incorporated from its parent and is domiciled in a foreign country. A bank can establish a foreign subsidiary by owning more than 50 percent of its voting stock, directly or through the bank's affiliates, or by demonstrating its control in other ways. The FRB's Regulation K requires a member bank to hold its interest in a foreign non-banking subsidiary through an Edge Act or Agreement Corporation. In contrast, a member bank may own a foreign bank directly.

A bank might choose to own a foreign subsidiary rather than a foreign branch for several reasons. The subsidiary structure helps protect a parent bank from the subsidiary's legal liabilities. In some countries that prohibit foreign branching, a bank can operate a financial subsidiary. These subsidiaries can often engage in broader activities than a branch. For example, if permitted by local law, a subsidiary generally might perform merchant banking activities, whereas a branch could not perform under either U.S. or foreign law. Whereas a branch is precluded from underwriting many types of securities, a merchant bank may be able to underwrite any type. Initially, subsidiaries were set up to attract retail business, such as deposits and loans, as well as for trade finance. Now, subsidiaries are often specialized entities that conduct activities that the parent bank cannot.

For foreign subsidiaries, the bank should have on file (in addition to audited financial information prepared for management):

- Reports prepared in conformance with the FRB's Regulation K, 12 CFR 211.

- Reports prepared for and obtained from foreign regulatory authorities.

- Information on the country's cultural and legal influences upon banking activities, current economic condition, anticipated relaxation or strengthening of capital or exchange controls, fiscal policy, political goals, and risk of expropriation.

A foreign subsidiary which is a financial subsidiary is subject to 12 CFR 5.39, but not Regulation K.

International Banking Facilities

An International Banking Facility (IBF) is an alternative to an offshore branch or subsidiary. IBFs are financial vehicles designed to enhance the competitive position of banking institutions in the United States by permitting them to obtain, through an IBF, similar treatment afforded to offshore banking offices. An IBF is simply a set of accounts segregated on the books and records of a depository institution. Implemented by amendments to the FRB's regulations 12 CFR 204 and 217, IBFs generally accept deposits from and advance funds to foreign customers, other IBFs, and the entity establishing the IBF. Foreign customers include, but are not limited to, residents of countries other than the United States, foreign affiliates of U.S. corporations, foreign banks, foreign government agencies, and quasi-governmental international organizations such as the United Nations. Both the deposits of and extensions of credit to foreign residents and foreign affiliates of U.S. corporations may be used only to support operations outside the United States. In general, such funds are exempt from reserve requirements and Federal Deposit Insurance Corporation (FDIC) assessments, and have tax advantages in some states.

Because IBFs have these advantages, an IBF has a lower cost of funds than an insured bank providing identical services. Using an IBF, a national bank can gain funding opportunities in international markets without having to establish a foreign branch. Subject to certain restrictions, IBFs have permitted banks to become involved in the Eurocurrency market from domestic bases. However, the relative advantage with respect to deposit reserves was largely eliminated when the FRB relaxed the deposit reserve requirements in the early 1990s. Another incentive to use IBFs is that they may be exempted from state taxes.

An IBF may purchase eligible assets from the entity establishing the IBF (subject to Eurocurrency reserve requirements), or it may sell such assets to that entity. Also, the entity may use the credit extended by the IBF

---

domestically in the United States.[6] IBFs may also book off-balance-sheet items, provided the customer is eligible under, and the transactions comply with, applicable regulation.

No application and no approval are required to establish an IBF. An institution that wants to establish an IBF is required only to notify the FRB in its district at least 14 days before the first reserve computation period during which it intends to accept IBF deposits.

Community Development Investments

Pursuant to 12 USC 24(Eleventh), a bank is authorized to make investments designed primarily to promote the public welfare, including the welfare of low- and moderate-income communities and families, such as by providing housing, services, or jobs. The regulation that implements this statutory authority is 12 CFR 24.

Community development investments authorized under the statute and regulation include those that support affordable housing, economic development and job creation, community and economic development entities, and other public welfare purposes.

Public Welfare Requirement

A bank's investment under the regulation must meet at least one of the four following criteria: (1) it must primarily benefit low- and moderate-income individuals, (2) it must primarily benefit low- and moderate-income areas, (3) it must primarily benefit other areas targeted by a government entity for redevelopment, or (4) it must otherwise be considered a "qualified investment" under 12 CFR 25.23 (of the Community Reinvestment Act (CRA) regulation). Examples of investments that would meet the public welfare standard are listed under 12 CFR 24.6.

Investment Limits

A bank's aggregate outstanding investments and commitments under 12 CFR 24 may not exceed 5 percent of its capital and surplus, unless the bank is at

---

[6] Based on interpretation by the attorneys of the Federal Reserve System.

least adequately capitalized and the OCC determines, by its written approval of the bank's proposed investment, that a higher amount will pose no significant risk to the deposit insurance fund. In no case may a bank's aggregate outstanding investments and commitments under 12 CFR 24 exceed 10 percent of its capital and surplus.

When calculating the aggregate amount of its outstanding investments under this regulation, a national bank should follow GAAP, unless the OCC, in writing, directs or permits otherwise for prudential or safety and soundness reasons.

A bank may not make an investment under 12 CFR 24 that would expose the bank to unlimited liability.

Types of Investments

A bank may make public welfare investments by purchasing an interest in a community and economic development entity (CEDE) or by investing directly in a community development project.[7]

A CEDE is an entity that makes investments or conducts activities that primarily benefit low- and moderate-income individuals, low- and moderate-income areas, or other areas targeted by a governmental entity for redevelopment. An entity that makes qualifying investments under the CRA regulation is also deemed a CEDE. The following is a partial list of the types of entities that may be CEDEs:

- National bank community development corporation subsidiaries.

- Private or nonbank community development corporations.

- CDFI Fund-certified community development financial institutions (CDFIs) or community development entities.

- Limited liability companies or limited partnerships.

- Community development loan funds or lending consortia.

---

[7] 12 CFR 24 allows national banks' public welfare investments in a variety of structures as described in the definition of a "community and economic development entity," under 12 CFR 24.3(c), and in the definition of a "community development project," under 12 CFR 24.3(d).

- Community development real estate investment trusts.

- Business development companies.

- Community development closed-end mutual funds.

- Nondiversified closed-end investment companies.

- Community development venture or equity capital funds.

A community development project (CD project) is a project whose investment meets the public welfare requirements of 12 CFR 24.

Notification and Approval Processes

After-the-Fact Notice

An eligible bank may make public welfare investments without first notifying or obtaining the approval of the OCC if the bank follows prescribed after-the-fact notice procedures. To provide an after-the-fact notice of an investment, an eligible bank must submit a completed form CD-1[8] within 10 working days after it makes the investment, to Director, Community Development Division, OCC, 250 E Street, SW, Washington, DC 20219.

To be eligible for the after-the-fact notice process, a bank:

- Must be well capitalized, as defined in 12 CFR 6.4,

- Must have a composite rating of 1 or 2 under the Uniform Financial Institutions Rating System,

- Must have a CRA rating of "outstanding" or "satisfactory," and

- Must not be subject to a cease and desist order, consent order, formal written agreement, or Prompt Corrective Action directive, or, if subject to any such order, agreement or directive, must be informed in writing by the OCC that the bank may be treated as an "eligible bank" for purposes of 12 CFR 24.

In addition, the bank must certify that its investment is in compliance with the public welfare and investment limit requirements of 12 CFR 24.

A bank may not provide an after-the-fact notice of an investment if:

---

[8] Available under the "Community Affairs" link at http://www.occ.treas.gov.

- The bank's aggregate outstanding investments and commitments under 12 CFR 24 are greater than or equal to 5 percent of its capital and surplus, unless the OCC previously has determined, by written approval, that a higher amount would pose no significant risk to the deposit insurance fund;

- The investment involves properties carried on the bank's books as "other real estate owned"; or

- The OCC determines, in published guidance, that the investment is inappropriate for after-the-fact notice.

Investments Requiring Prior OCC Approval

If a bank or its proposed investment does not meet the requirements for after-the-fact notice, the bank shall submit an investment proposal to Director, Community Development. Unless otherwise notified in writing by the OCC, the proposed investment is deemed approved after 30 calendar days.

The OCC may impose one or more conditions on its approval of an investment under 12 CFR 24. All approvals are subject to the condition that a national bank must conduct the approved activity in a manner consistent with the OCC's published guidance on the activity.

Required Information for a Part 24 Submission

Both the after-the-fact notice and the investment proposal must include the following items (the bank may use the form CD-1 to satisfy this requirement):

- A description of the bank's investment;

- The dollar amount of the investment;

- The percentage of the bank's capital and surplus represented by the bank's investment that is the subject of the after-the-fact notice or investment proposal;

- The percentage of the bank's capital and surplus represented by the bank's aggregate outstanding public welfare investments and commitments, including the investment proposal or the after-the-fact notice investment; and

- A statement from the bank certifying compliance with the public welfare requirements and investment limits of 12 CFR 24.

Each bank should maintain in its files information adequate to demonstrate that its investment meets the public welfare standards, including, when applicable, the criteria of the CRA regulation. The bank's files should also substantiate that the bank is otherwise in compliance with the requirements of this part.

Remedial Action

If the OCC determines that a CEDE, CD project, or other public welfare investment violates a law or regulation, is inconsistent with the safe and sound operation of the bank, or poses a significant risk to the bank deposit insurance fund, the OCC will require the bank to take appropriate remedial action. The bank could be required to reduce or withdraw its investment in the CEDE or CD project.

Related Interests of Insiders

A "related interest" is simply a type of related organization defined for purposes of the statute and regulations that govern a bank's loans to its "insiders." See 12 USC 375b, as well as 122 CFR 31 and Regulation O, 12 CFR 215.[9] The statute and regulations apply restrictions to, among other things, a bank's loans to any of its "principal shareholders" (defined for these purposes as natural persons who control a bank) and any "related interests " of a principal shareholder. A "related interest" is generally deemed to be a company that the principal shareholder controls. There is some overlap between insider-lending laws and affiliate transactions laws. Many related interests of a bank's principal shareholder would also be "affiliates" of the bank. The "Insider Activities" booklet of the Comptroller's Handbook contains additional information on the insider-lending restrictions. The following section provides additional information on transactions with affiliates.

---

[9] Regulation O applies to insiders of banks, which include principal shareholders, directors, and executive officers, and their related interests. The "Insider Activities" booklet of the Comptroller's Handbook contains additional information on transactions with insiders.

Transactions with Affiliates

Sections 23A and 23B of the Federal Reserve Act (12 USC 371c and 371c-1), and their implementing regulation, Regulation W (12 CFR 223), restrict a bank's transactions with its affiliates in order to safeguard the interests of banks and prevent abuses by banks' affiliates.[10]

Sections 23A and Regulation W define "affiliate" to include:

- Any company that controls the bank, and any other company that is controlled by the company that controls the bank.[11]

- An insured depository institution subsidiary of the bank.

- Any company that is controlled directly or indirectly by a trust or otherwise, by or for the benefit of shareholders who beneficially or otherwise control, directly or indirectly, by trust or otherwise, the bank or any company that controls the bank.

- Any company a majority of whose directors, trustees, or general partners constitute a majority of the persons holding these offices with the bank or any company that controls the bank.

- Any company, including a real estate investment trust, which is sponsored and advised on a contractual basis by the bank or any subsidiary or affiliate of the bank.

- Any investment company for which a bank or any subsidiary or affiliate thereof serves as an investment adviser.

- Any other investment fund for which the bank or any subsidiary or affiliate serves as an investment adviser, if the bank and its subsidiaries and affiliates together own or control more than 5 percent of any class of voting securities or of the equity capital of the fund.

- A financial subsidiary of the bank.[12]

---

[10] Users of this booklet should not rely on this synopsis as a complete discussion of Regulation W, and are urged to closely review the regulation for a full understanding of its requirements and restrictions.

[11] Generally, "control" for purposes of sections 23A and 23B means the power to vote 25 percent or more of any class of voting securities or to control in any manner the election of directors or trustees of the company. This control threshold is lower than the one in the definition of control in section 221a. Certain other relationships may constitute control, as well.

- Any company in which the bank's holding company owns or controls, directly, indirectly, or acting through one or more other persons, 15 percent or more of the equity capital pursuant to the merchant banking or insurance investment authority of the GLBA, subject to certain exceptions.

- Any partnership for which the bank or any subsidiary or affiliate of the bank serves as a general partner or for which the bank or any subsidiary or affiliate of the bank causes any director, official, or employee of the bank or its subsidiary or affiliate to serve as a general partner.

- Any company that the FRB (by regulation or order) or OCC (by order) deems to be an "affiliate."

Under section 23B, the term "affiliate" has the same meaning as it does in section 23A, except that it excludes insured depository institutions.

Transactions between a bank and the following companies are exempt from the restrictions on transactions with affiliates:

- An uninsured depository institution subsidiary of the bank.[13]

- Most subsidiaries of the bank that are not insured depository institutions. Subsidiaries that *are* treated as affiliates include financial subsidiaries and subsidiaries (including uninsured depository institutions) that are also controlled by one or more affiliates of the bank that are not insured depository institutions. (In addition, as noted above, the OCC and the FRB can determine that an otherwise exempt subsidiary should be treated as an affiliate).

- Any company engaged solely in holding bank premises.

---

[12] However, organizations that are considered financial subsidiaries solely because they engage in the sale of insurance as agent or broker in a manner that is not permitted for national banks are not considered to be "financial subsidiaries" for purposes of Regulation W.

[13] When the subsidiary bank is uninsured, it is not treated as an affiliate of the parent bank for purposes of either section 23A or section 23B, but instead is treated as an exempt operating subsidiary from the perspective of the *parent bank*. Note, however, that from the perspective of the *uninsured subsidiary bank*, its parent bank *is* treated as an affiliate, and thus the restrictions of sections 23A and 23B apply to transactions with the parent bank, unless an exemption, such as the sister-bank exemption, is available.

- Any company engaged solely in conducting a safe deposit business.

- Any company engaged solely in holding obligations of the United States, its agencies, or any obligations fully guaranteed by the United States or its agencies.

- Subject to certain limitations and conditions, any company acquired in collecting debt previously contracted.

From a practical standpoint, examples of the most prevalent types of affiliates for purposes of applying the affiliate transaction rules are the bank's parent company, nonbank subsidiaries of the bank's holding company, and entities that are controlled by a person who is also a controlling owner of the bank, including chain banks.

Restrictions

Covered Transactions

Transactions governed by section 23A are referred to as "covered transactions." Covered transactions are:

- Loans and extensions of credit to affiliates.

- Purchases of assets from affiliates.

- An investment in securities issued by an affiliate.

- The acceptance of securities issued by an affiliate as collateral for a loan or extension of credit to any person.

- The issuance of a guarantee, acceptance, or letter of credit (including an endorsement or standby letter of credit) on behalf of an affiliate, a confirmation of a letter of credit issued by the affiliate, and certain cross-affiliate netting arrangements.[14]

Attribution Rule

Section 23A provides that any covered transaction between a bank and an unaffiliated third party generally must be attributed to any affiliate that receives the proceeds or direct benefit of that transaction. For example, if a

---

[14] This category of covered transactions, together with loans and extensions of credit, is referred to as "credit transactions" in Regulation W and this booklet.

bank makes a loan to its customer for the purpose of making a purchase from the bank's retail affiliate or for the purpose of purchasing securities from an affiliated mutual fund or broker-dealer, the loan is generally treated as if it was made directly to the affiliate.

Regulation W provides a specific exception to the attribution rule for certain agency transactions. If a bank extends credit to an unaffiliated third party that uses the credit to purchase an asset through an affiliate of the bank, the bank is not considered to have extended credit to the affiliate under the attribution rule, provided that the affiliate is acting exclusively as an agent or broker in the transaction and the asset purchased is not issued, underwritten, or sold as principal by any affiliate of the bank. [15]

Certain other transactions, while treated as transactions with an affiliate under the attribution rule, nonetheless receive an exemption from the quantitative limits and the collateral requirements (described below). These exempted transactions include:

- An affiliate's retention of a portion of the proceeds of an extension of credit as a brokerage commission, agency fee, or riskless principal markup, if such commission, fee, or markup is substantially the same as (or lower than) those prevailing at the time for comparable transactions with or involving nonaffiliates, in accordance with section 23B's market-terms requirements.

- An extension of credit by a bank to an unaffiliated third party to purchase a security through a securities affiliate of the bank, provided that the securities affiliate is acting exclusively as a riskless principal in the transaction, the security is not issued, underwritten, or sold as principal (other than as riskless principal) by any affiliate of the bank, and any compensation received by the affiliate from the proceeds of the extension of credit meets the market-terms standard in section 23B, as implemented by Regulation W.

- An extension of credit by a bank to an unaffiliated third party to purchase a security from or through a securities affiliate of the bank, if

---

[15] Any agency fee, brokerage commission, or other compensation retained by the affiliate from the proceeds of the extension of credit would be treated as an extension of credit to the affiliate. However, the receipt of such compensation may qualify for the exemption for brokerage commissions described below.

the extension of credit is made in accordance with a pre-existing line of credit that was not established in contemplation of the purchase of securities from or through an affiliate.

- An extension of credit by a bank to an unaffiliated third party to purchase a product or service from an affiliate using a "general purpose credit card" issued by the bank.

These exempted transactions remain subject to the safety and soundness requirements and market-terms requirements.

Quantitative Limits

Except for transactions with financial subsidiaries, a bank's covered transactions with any single affiliate may not exceed 10 percent of the bank's capital and surplus.[16] The aggregate of covered transactions with all affiliates (including financial subsidiaries) may not exceed 20 percent of the bank's capital and surplus. A bank's transactions with its financial subsidiaries are not subject to the 10 percent limit for a single affiliate, but are included in the 20 percent aggregate limit for all affiliates.

In general, unless an exemption is available (see "Exemptions"), a bank must observe the quantitative limits when engaging in a covered transaction with a nonbank affiliate. Thus, a bank's purchase of assets from its holding company, or a subsidiary of that holding company, usually may not exceed 10 percent of the bank's capital and surplus.

Qualitative Restrictions

Unless an exemption is available, credit transactions with affiliates must be collateralized, and purchases of "low-quality assets" generally are prohibited. In addition, all covered transactions (whether or not exempted from other restrictions of Regulation W) must be consistent with safe and sound banking practices.

---

[16] Capital and surplus is defined in 12 CFR 223.3(d) as Tier 1 and Tier 2 capital included in the bank's risk-based capital plus the balance of the allowance for loan and lease losses not included in Tier 2 capital for the purposes of calculating risk-based capital. It also includes the amount of any investment by a member bank in a financial subsidiary that counts as a covered transaction and is required to be deducted from the bank's capital for regulatory capital purposes.

Collateral Requirements

A credit transaction with an affiliate must be secured by collateral having a market value that complies with the schedule set forth in section 23A:

- 100 percent of the amount of the transaction if the collateral is obligations of or fully guaranteed by the U.S. government or its agencies; notes, drafts, bill of exchange, or eligible acceptances; or a segregated, earmarked deposit account meeting certain requirements;

- 110 percent if the collateral is obligations of any state or its political subdivisions;

- 120 percent if the collateral is other debt instruments, including loans and other receivables; or

- 130 percent if the collateral is stock, leases, or other property.

The bank must ensure that any required collateral that is retired or amortized is replaced by eligible collateral to maintain the required percentage. Low-quality assets, any securities issued by an affiliate, equity securities issued by the bank, debt securities issued by the bank that represent regulatory capital of the bank, guarantees, letters of credit (or similar instruments), and intangible assets (unless approved by the FRB) are not eligible collateral.

A bank must maintain a perfected security interest in collateral that secures a covered transaction. If the bank does not obtain a first-priority security interest in the collateral, it must make a prescribed deduction from the collateral's value to reflect the senior interests.

Certain credit transactions, including purchases of an affiliate's debt securities from a nonaffiliate in a *bona fide* secondary market transaction, are exempt from collateral requirements.

Transfers of Low-Quality Assets

A bank's purchase of low-quality assets from an affiliate is generally prohibited (although the prohibition does not apply (1) if the bank had committed to purchase the asset, pursuant to an independent credit evaluation, before the asset was acquired by the affiliate, or (2) to certain renewals of loan participations). An affiliate may *donate* a low-quality asset to a bank so long as the bank does not provide consideration (payment or liabilities assumed). The term "low-quality asset" in regulation W includes:

- An asset (including a security) classified as "substandard," "doubtful," or "loss," or treated as "other assets especially mentioned" or "other transfer risk problems";[17]

- An asset in nonaccrual status;

- An asset 30 days past due; or

- An asset whose terms have been renegotiated or compromised because the obligor's financial condition has deteriorated.

- An asset acquired in satisfaction of a debt previously contracted and not yet reviewed in an examination or inspection.

Safety and Soundness

As noted above, all covered transactions with affiliates, even those exempted from other restrictions of Regulation W, must be on terms and conditions that are consistent with safe and sound banking practices.

Section 23B and the "Arm's-Length Requirement"

Section 23B requires that transactions between a bank (or its subsidiary) and its affiliates be conducted on terms and under conditions that are at least as favorable to the bank as those prevailing at the time for comparable transactions with nonaffiliated companies. A bank may pay no more than fair market value for the assets it purchases and must receive at least fair market value for the assets it sells. For purposes of section 23B, Regulation W excludes from the definition of "affiliate" all insured depository institutions.

Transactions with Insured and Uninsured Bank Affiliates

Regulation W provides that a bank's covered transactions with an *insured* bank affiliate may be eligible for certain exemptions from the restrictions of

---

[17] The asset can be classified either in the most recent report of examination of an affiliate or in any internal classification system, and classifications include ratings substantially equivalent to the classification categories used in Regulation W.

section 23A and Regulation W, such as the Bank Merger Act ("BMA") and sister-bank exemptions. However, a bank's transactions with an *uninsured* bank affiliate do not qualify for most exemptions from section 23A and thus are generally subject to all of section 23A's restrictions, unless the uninsured bank is a subsidiary of the bank and is not controlled by an affiliate of the bank that is not an insured depository institution.

With respect to section 23B, Regulation W provides that *insured* banks are not considered affiliates at all, and thus transactions by a bank with an insured depository institution are not covered by section 23B. *Uninsured* sister depository institutions, however, *are* treated as affiliates subject to the arm's-length standard and other applicable restrictions of section 23B. As is the case under 23A, however, a bank's transactions with a subsidiary uninsured bank are generally exempt from section 23B.

Exemptions from sections 23A and 23B are discussed in more detail below; however, banks considering engaging in affiliate transactions may wish to consult with the OCC in advance because of the complexity of the exemptions.

Exemptions

Sister Bank and BMA

The sister-bank[18] and BMA exemptions are available to permit a bank to engage in covered transactions with insured affiliated depository institutions subject only to the safety and soundness requirement in section 23A and, in the case of the sister-bank exemption, the prohibition against the purchase of low-quality assets.[19] For example, an insured bank may sell its operating subsidiary to an insured sister bank, even if the purchase price exceeds 10 percent of the acquiring bank's capital and surplus, provided the operating subsidiary has no low-quality assets and the transaction is not unsafe or unsound. If one of the transacting banks is uninsured, however, the "sister-bank" and BMA exemptions may not be available.

---

[18] Banks are considered "sister banks" if the same holding company controls 80 percent or more of the voting securities of each of the banks.

[19] A similar parent/subsidiary bank exemption is available when a bank controls 80 percent or more of the voting securities of an insured depository institution or when the latter controls 80 percent or more of the bank's voting securities.

Internal Corporate Reorganizations

Certain "internal corporate reorganizations" are exempted from the collateral requirements and quantitative limits of section 23A, but not from the low-quality-asset prohibition, the safety and soundness requirement, and section 23B. Several conditions must be satisfied in order for this exemption to be available. These conditions are:

- The transactions must be part of an internal corporate reorganization of a holding company involving the transfer of all or substantially all of the shares or assets of an affiliate or of a division of an affiliate;

- The bank must provide advance notice to the OCC and the FRB, including a description of the primary business of the affiliate and an indication of the proposed date of the transfer;

- The bank's top-tier holding company must commit to the OCC and the FRB (and carry through on its commitment) to fully reimburse the bank on a quarterly basis with respect to any assets that become low-quality during the first two years after the transfer, either by making cash contributions to the bank or by purchasing the low-quality assets;[20]

- A majority of the bank's board of directors must review and approve the transactions in advance;

- The value of the covered transaction, when aggregated with any other transactions undertaken pursuant to this internal corporate reorganization exemption during the previous 12 months, must represent less than 10 percent of the bank's capital and surplus (if the OCC approves in advance, the value may represent up to 25 percent of the bank's capital and surplus); and

- The holding company and all of its subsidiary member banks and depository institutions must be well capitalized and well managed both before and after consummation of the transfer.

De Novo Banks

Regulation W exempts asset purchases by *de novo* banks from section 23A's collateral requirements, quantitative limits, and low-quality asset prohibition,

---

[20] The amount of such cash payments or purchase must equal the book value of the low-quality assets plus any write-downs taken.

and from section 23B's market-terms requirement (but not from section 23A's safety and soundness requirement), provided that the OCC has approved the asset purchase in writing in connection with its review of the formation of the new bank.

Step Transactions

Regulation W exempts "step transactions" from the provisions of section 23A (except for the safety and soundness requirement), though not from section 23B. A step transaction occurs when a bank acquires the securities of a company within one business day (this time limit may be extended by the OCC) after the company first becomes an affiliate as a result of its acquisition by an affiliate of the bank. The acquiring bank must acquire all of the shares that were acquired by the transferring affiliate. For example, a step transaction exists when a bank's holding company acquires 100 percent of the shares of an unaffiliated company and then immediately transfers all of the shares of that company to its subsidiary bank. Certain conditions must be satisfied in order to qualify for the step transaction exemption, including notice by the bank to both the OCC and the FRB (at or before the time when the transferred company first becomes an affiliate) that the bank intends to acquire the company.

Intraday Extensions of Credit

Regulation W exempts "intraday extensions of credit" from section 23A, except for the safety and soundness requirement. An intraday extension of credit is defined as an extension of credit to an affiliate that the lending bank expects to be repaid, sold, or terminated, or to qualify for a complete exemption from Regulation W, by the end of the bank's U.S. business day. The availability of this exemption is conditioned on the bank's establishment and maintenance of certain specified policies and procedures reasonably designed to manage the credit exposure arising from the bank's intraday extensions of credit in a safe and sound manner.

Other Exemptions

Other exemptions from the limits of section 23A include purchasing marketable securities, purchasing municipal securities, and certain riskless principal transactions. All of these exemptions are subject to certain requirements or limits. Regulation W also modified certain exemptions from section 23A that pre-dated Regulation W, such as section 23A's exemption for purchasing liquid assets and the regulatory exemption for purchasing extensions of credit from an affiliate (formerly found at 12 CFR 250.250). In addition, Regulation W creates specific new exemptions from section 23B's requirements.

Board and Management Responsibilities

A bank's board of directors' primary duty is to protect the interests of the *bank*. A bank's use of related organizations to perform bank functions, provide products and services to customers, or otherwise achieve its strategic goals does not diminish the responsibility of the board of directors and management to ensure that both the relationships and the provision of products and services are conducted in a safe and sound manner and serve the bank's best interests. A bank's board and management can best meet this responsibility by implementing a corporate governance structure that provides for effective policies and controls systems over relationships with related organizations and that insulates the directors and management from pressure to subordinate the interests of the bank to those of the corporate parent or other related organizations.

Policies and Control Systems

As mentioned earlier, related organizations can subject the bank to a variety of risks. Accordingly, the bank's relationships with its related organizations should be subject to robust risk management and control systems. Policies and procedures are of particular importance when the bank conducts new or complex activities within a subsidiary or affiliate. Among other things, the board's risk management system should include guidelines and controls for related organizations governing:

- All transactions with related organizations, to ensure that they are carried out at arm's length and in the bank's best interests.

- The performance of functions or services on behalf of the bank, such as information processing, internal audit, and risk management.

- The formation or acquisition of new related organizations, and any new activities conducted by existing related organizations. These policies are especially important when a new related organization offers new services to the bank or its customers.

- Management information systems, including independent audit reports. Such information should document the nature and financial status of related organizations.

- Transactions with affiliates and lending to insiders' related interests.

- Actual and potential conflicts of interest, to ensure that they are disclosed and controlled.

- Tying the availability of a product or service to obtaining a product or service from an affiliate of the bank, to ensure that no impermissible tying occurs.

- Sharing of customer information with the related organization, to ensure that such information sharing is permitted and that the customer information remains confidential.

- Sharing of employees or office space, to ensure that such arrangements comply with legal requirements and do not harm the bank or cause customer confusion.

- Transparency and disclosure, to ensure that shareholders and regulators understand the bank's relationship with its affiliates and other related organizations, as well as the risks these relationships pose.

The formality and extent of a bank's risk management and control systems will depend on the number, size, organizational and ownership characteristics, business activities, and operational diversity and complexity of its related organizations. (For more information on these topics, see the "Internal Control" booklet of the Comptroller's Handbook.)

Maintaining Independence

The board's duty of loyalty takes on added significance when a bank is a subsidiary of a diversified holding company that owns numerous nonbank companies as well as other banks. The board and management of a bank that is part of a holding company may have a different operating environment than an independent bank does. When there are multiple related companies with different business purposes, a bank's board must ensure that the activities of the other related companies do not conflict with the bank's best interests.

The bank's board should not relinquish control of bank activities or functions that are outsourced to, or performed by, the BHC or other related organizations. The board's corporate governance practices should require a careful review of holding company policies and procedures that affect the bank, ensuring that they adequately serve the bank. Strong board oversight is particularly important when bank functions, such as risk management systems, are centralized within a diversified holding company or are outsourced to another related organization.

The bank's board should regularly monitor the impact of holding company policies that affect the bank. If concerned that the holding company is engaging in practices that may harm the bank or are otherwise inappropriate, the bank's board should notify the holding company and obtain modifications. If the holding company board does not address the bank's concerns, bank directors should dissent on the record and should consider action to protect the bank. If necessary, it should hire an independent legal counsel or accountant. The board also may communicate its concerns to the OCC.

Unsafe and unsound activities of nonbank subsidiaries of the bank's holding company may adversely affect the bank's condition and reputation. A bank's board and management must be appropriately informed of the condition and activities of all holding company subsidiaries.

Other Issues

Management and Other Fees

Sound corporate governance practices covering related organizations include developing policies and controls addressing the payment of fees to related parties. Arrangements in which a subsidiary bank obtains goods and services from the parent holding company or other affiliate may benefit the bank since the supplier may offer lower costs because of economies of scale. Furthermore, banks may be able to purchase a package of services that otherwise might not be available. Fees paid by the bank to the parent or other affiliates should have a direct relationship to, and be based solely on, the fair value of goods and services provided. Fees should compensate the affiliated supplier only for providing goods and services that meet the legitimate needs of the bank. Affiliates should be qualified to provide those goods and services.

In general, the affiliated supplier will decide on the amount to be charged by using one of three methods:

- Reimbursement for cost of goods or services.

- Cost plus a reasonable profit margin.

- Comparative fair-market value.

In determining the cost of the goods or services, the parent or affiliate service provider may recover overhead expenses to the extent that they are a legitimate and integral part of the goods or services being provided. Overhead may include salaries and wages, occupancy cost, utilities, payroll taxes, supplies, and advertising.

Any of the three methods previously mentioned may be acceptable provided that the bank can substantiate that the fees paid are reasonable for the value received. Basing fees on costs may be the most common approach since market comparisons often are difficult to obtain. A bank holding company may be able to offer a number of services on a cost basis to a subsidiary bank, any one of which might be contracted elsewhere for less. The justification for such an arrangement would be that, in the aggregate, the services may be cost effective or may produce economies of scale for the entire organization. Nevertheless, having one or more subsidiary banks pay excessive fees for goods and services to subsidize other unprofitable operations is not an acceptable practice and may violate section 23B of the Federal Reserve Act.

Each bank should retain satisfactory records that substantiate the value of goods and services received, their benefit to the bank, and their cost efficiencies. Those records should be available for review by examiners.

If excessive management or other fees are paid to affiliated organizations, the board of directors is responsible for taking corrective action, which may include requiring restitution. Prepayment of fees for services not yet received may violate section 23A of the Federal Reserve Act.

Generally, a national bank may not enter into a written or oral contract with any person to provide products or services to or for the benefit of the bank if the performance of such contract would adversely affect the safety and soundness of the institution. See 12 USC 1831g.

Accounting

Policies and control systems should ensure that accounting treatment for controlling and noncontrolling investments is appropriate. Ownership interests in related organizations should be accounted for in accordance with GAAP. Depending on the circumstances, the bank may account for its investment on a consolidated basis by the equity or the cost method of accounting. When determining which accounting method is appropriate, the bank should consider the entity's legal structure, the bank's percent of ownership, and how much control the bank has over the entity.

Consolidated financial statements combine the assets, liabilities, revenues, and expenses of the entity with those of the reporting bank. For the purposes of such a statement, the bank and its subsidiaries are a single economic entity. Generally, all significant majority-owned subsidiary corporations must be consolidated into the financial statements of the parent bank unless the subsidiary is covered by one of the limited exceptions included in the "General Instructions to the Consolidated Reports of Condition and Income" (call report instructions).

Under the *equity method,* the bank's investment in the entity, which is originally recorded at cost, is adjusted periodically to record the bank's share of the entity's earnings and losses. Dividends and similar distributions received from the entity reduce the bank's recorded investment. If the parent owns between 20 percent and 50 percent of the outstanding voting stock of a subsidiary, it is generally presumed to have significant influence over operating and financial policies of the related entity and the investment is accounted for under the equity method.

Under the *cost method,* the bank's investment remains recorded at cost. Income is recognized only as dividends are received. If the parent does not exercise significant influence (it owns less than 20 percent of the outstanding voting stock of the subsidiary), the cost method is used.

Investments in unincorporated interests, such as partnerships or joint ventures, should be accounted for based on the substance of the partnership or joint venture agreement. If the bank has control over the entity,

consolidation would be appropriate. Noncontrolling partnership interests are generally accounted for under the equity method of accounting.
In certain entities, the equity investors (legal owners) do not have the characteristics of ownership (such as controlling financial interest or sufficient equity at risk). In such cases, another party generally provides the financial support that will absorb some or all of the entity's expected losses if they occur. Such an entity referred to as "variable interest entity" (VIE). In these situations, GAAP requires that the party at risk consolidate the VIE in its financial statements

Accounting guidance for ownership interests is included in the instructions to the call reports. Detailed requirements are included in the general instructions, the "Subsidiaries" entry of the glossary instructions, and the instructions to Schedule RC–M. This guidance is consistent with GAAP as set forth in Statement of Financial Accounting Standards 94, American Institute of Certified Public Accountants (AICPA) Accounting Research Bulletin 51, AICPA Accounting Principles Board Opinion 18, AICPA Statement of Position 78–9, and Financial Accounting Standards Board (FASB) Interpretations 35 and 46.

Tying — Federal Prohibitions

Control systems should ensure that the bank does not impermissibly condition the availability or price of one product on a requirement that the customer also obtain a product from an affiliate of the bank. The tying statute, 12 USC 1972, and its implementing regulation, 12 CFR 225.7, set forth prohibitions, but also provide some exceptions to the statutory tying restrictions. The exceptions permit certain tying arrangements for national banks and are applicable to national bank operating subsidiaries.

For purposes of the federal tying prohibitions, when a national bank and its financial subsidiary are part of a bank holding company, the subsidiary is considered a subsidiary of the holding company and not the bank, as provided in 12 USC 1971 (also see 12 CFR 5.39(h)(6)). Thus, the general tying restrictions applicable to national banks and their operating subsidiaries are not applicable to financial subsidiaries.

The term "affiliate" in the tying context refers to any company or natural person that controls a bank and any company that is controlled by such company or person (other than the bank itself). Any subsidiary of such a company is treated as a subsidiary of a bank holding company. The tying restrictions apply to *banks*; they *generally* do not apply to arrangements imposed by an affiliate of a bank. The Board of Governors of the Federal Reserve System has authority to interpret and grant exceptions to the tying statute. Banks and their affiliates also are subject to anti-tying standards under the general antitrust laws. These standards are premised on finding an actual anti-competitive effect of the tying arrangement, however.

The statutory and regulatory exceptions to tying allow a bank to restrict the availability or to vary the price of any bank product on the condition that the customer obtain a "traditional bank product" from the bank or an affiliate of the bank. For example, a bank may condition the availability or price of a particular loan on a requirement that the customer maintain a specified amount of deposits with the bank or its affiliates. This condition is allowed because the exception for traditional bank products includes deposits.

Further, the tying restrictions do not prevent a bank from requiring a customer to obtain acceptable credit-related insurance as a condition for loan approval. In such circumstances, the bank may inform the customer that insurance is available from the bank or its affiliates and may provide instructions on how the customer can obtain additional information. The bank is prohibited, however, from *requiring* the customer to purchase the insurance from the bank, its subsidiaries, or any of its affiliates as a condition of granting the loan, because the insurance is not a traditional bank product. Accordingly, the bank should clearly inform the customer that: (1) he or she need not purchase the insurance from the bank, its subsidiary, or an affiliate; (2) the insurance is available through brokers or agents other than the bank; and (3) the customer's choice of insurance provider will not affect the bank's credit decision or credit terms.

The bank's controls system should include:

- Training bank employees about the tying prohibitions, including providing examples of prohibited practices.
- Reviewing training, marketing, audit, and compliance programs, and updating any policies and procedures to reflect changes in products, services, or applicable law.

- Reviewing customer files to determine whether the bank has impermissibly conditioned any extension of credit on the customer obtaining another product or service from the bank or its affiliates.

- Monitoring incentives, such as commissions and fee-splitting arrangements that may encourage tying.

- Responding to any customer allegations of prohibited tying arrangements.

Please refer to the FRB's issuance, "Anti-Tying Restrictions of Section 106 of the Bank Holding Company Act Amendments of 1970"; the OCC's paper, "Today's Credit Markets, Relationship Banking, and Tying" (September 2003); and OCC Bulletin 95–20, "Tying Restrictions," for additional guidance on permissible and prohibited tying arrangements.

Supervision of Related Organizations

An assessment of the overall safety and soundness of a bank includes a review of related organizations to determine whether the activities of those related entities mitigate or increase the risks borne by the bank. Although the activities of, and risks posed by, related organizations may vary significantly, OCC's review of all types of related organizations will focus on three primary determinations:

- Whether the bank's risk management system and other corporate governance processes ensure that the interests of the bank are being properly regarded.

- The impact of the related organizations on the bank's reputation and franchise.

- The effect of the relationships on the bank's liquidity, earnings, and capital.

Examiners will review and evaluate the following aspects of the bank's governance of related organizations:

- Due diligence over the formation or acquisition of related organizations, particularly when a new related organization offers new services to the bank or its customers.

- Risk management functions, including audit and compliance, to ensure that risks posed by related organizations are appropriately identified, measured, monitored, and controlled.

- Controls to guard against conflicts of interest and the potential for dual loyalties, to ensure that dealings with related organizations are at arm's length and in the best interests of the bank.

- Monitoring for compliance with sections 23A and 23B and Regulation W, as well as for compliance with the federal anti-tying prohibitions.

- Controls to prevent the payment of inappropriate or unsubstantiated fees to related organizations.

- Transparency and adequacy of disclosure and reporting, to ensure that related organizations are identified and accounting treatment is appropriate.

If the bank's oversight system is appropriate in view of the nature and type of the activities conducted by the related organizations and the risks posed to the bank, a comprehensive analysis of each of the bank's related organizations may not be necessary.

With respect to operating subsidiaries, the OCC's supervisory process will continue to focus on reviewing and assessing the consolidated risk profile of a national bank. Operating subsidiaries are subject to the same supervision and regulation as the parent bank, except where otherwise provided by law or OCC regulation.

Functionally Regulated Affiliates and Subsidiaries

The Gramm–Leach–Bliley Act reaffirms the OCC's responsibility for evaluating the consolidated risk profiles of the individual national bank. It also establishes a regulatory framework for certain activities conducted within banks and through "functionally regulated affiliates and subsidiaries" (FRA). GLBA codifies this concept of "functional regulation," which recognizes the roles of the Securities and Exchange Commission, the Commodities Futures Trading Commission, and state insurance commissioners as the primary regulators of securities, commodities, and insurance activities, respectively. As national banks, their subsidiaries, and their affiliates become more involved in providing financial products and services that are functionally regulated, enhanced relationships between the OCC and other financial services regulators are increasingly important.

Although GLBA alters the OCC's responsibility for FRAs, the OCC remains the primary regulator of national banks, and thus maintains a vital interest in understanding all of the risks affecting national banks. The OCC's supervisory process will continue to focus on reviewing and assessing the consolidated risk profile of a national bank and its systems for monitoring and controlling risks, including risks posed by FRAs, such as risks that arise from intercompany transactions, reputational exposure from the activities of the FRAs, and compliance with laws under OCC's jurisdiction. This assessment embraces the OCC's supervision by risk approach by determining how frequently and extensively risks posed by FRAs should be analyzed. The assessment will be conducted at the bank level, and it is anticipated that, consistent with GLBA, the OCC's examination of FRAs will be infrequent.

The OCC communicates with the other regulatory agencies that supervise FRAs and functional lines of business within national banks. The OCC continues to develop processes and expand effective lines of communication between the agencies to facilitate the coordination of supervisory activities and the exchange of necessary information. For example, the OCC meets on regularly with the National Association of Insurance Commissioners to discuss the supervision of national bank insurance activities, as well as other relevant issues. In addition, the OCC has formal agreements with 49 state insurance regulators to share supervisory and enforcement information regarding bank insurance activities, as well as consumer complaints.

GLBA establishes new standards limiting the circumstances when the OCC can request reports from FRAs. Examiners first must request needed reports from the functional regulator. If such reports are insufficient or not made available, the OCC may seek reports directly from the FRA but only if they are necessary to assess:

- A material risk to the affiliated national bank;

- Compliance with a federal law the OCC has specific jurisdiction to enforce with respect to the FRA; or

- The system for monitoring and controlling financial and operational risks that may pose a threat to the safety and soundness of the affiliated national bank.

Similar limits apply to the direct examination of an FRA. The OCC may examine an FRA only when:

- There is reasonable cause to believe that the company is engaged in activities that pose a material risk to the affiliated national bank;

- After reviewing relevant reports, the OCC determines that an examination of the FRA is necessary to become adequately informed as to whether the company's system for monitoring and controlling operational and financial risks poses a threat to the safety and soundness of the affiliated national bank; or

- Based on reports and other information available, there is reasonable cause to believe that the company is not in compliance with federal law which the OCC has specific jurisdiction to enforce against the company, including provisions relating to transactions with affiliates, and the OCC cannot make such determination through examination of the affiliated national bank.

These limits do not apply when the functionally regulated activity is conducted directly by the bank. In that case, the functional regulator is responsible for interpreting and enforcing laws under its jurisdiction, and the activity is also subject to OCC supervision for safety and soundness reasons or because the OCC has separate statutory authority.

GLBA also does not restrict examiners from seeking information on an FRA from the bank or from sources other than the FRA. As a practical matter, OCC examiners can often obtain much of the information needed to assess the risks posed to the bank by FRAs or functionally regulated activities by regularly reviewing existing bank reports and meeting with compliance officers, auditors, risk officers, and other bank personnel.

In the case of FRAs, the examiner should consult with the appropriate deputy comptroller before requesting information from or conducting an examination of an FRA.

Whenever supervisory responsibility for an institution is shared with other regulatory agencies, the examiner-in-charge should follow the guidelines established in the "Bank Supervision Process" booklet of the *Comptroller's Handbook*. The OCC office that has supervisory authority for the lead national bank of a multibank holding company, the national bank affiliates of a multibank holding company with a lead state bank, or the lead national bank in a chain banking organization is responsible for coordinating the examinations of affiliated national banks in the organization with other regulatory agencies.

The table in appendix B illustrates the supervisory authority of the financial services regulators.

Identification of Related Organizations

To fully understand the risks related organizations pose to a bank, the examiner must determine the lines of business in which those related organizations engage, and determine the nature of the relationship between those related organizations and the bank. This information, coupled with information from other regulators, serves as the foundation for performing a consolidated risk analysis. Examiners should ask the bank to provide a list of its related organizations and identify those related organizations that have transactions with the bank. To facilitate the identification of related organizations, examiners should discuss related entities with various members of the bank's staff including management, legal staff, internal/external auditors, and the examiner liaison.

Additional sources of information include the bank's financial statement, the bank's annual report, bank holding company reports, shareholder lists, board of directors' meeting minutes, internal/external audit reports, OCC's corporate activity information system, OCC's supervisory information system, FRB holding company inspection reports, and state reports of bank holding company activities. Information about related organizations and interlocking directorates and officers also may be obtained from SEC forms 10–K and 10–Q or other required domestic and foreign regulatory reports.

Information on business interests of directors and principal officers of the bank can be obtained by reviewing information maintained in accordance with Regulation O. By reviewing this information, the examiner should be able to identify all credit relationships between the bank and related interests of those directors and officers, to determine whether the bank's loans to the related interests are within statutory limits, and to decide whether they are fair and reasonable from the bank's standpoint. Refer to the "Insider Activities" booklet of the *Comptroller's Handbook* for more information about directors, executive officers, principal shareholders, and their related interests.

Examiners may find it especially difficult to obtain information about foreign investments, statutory subsidiaries, and companies in which the bank has a noncontrolling interest. If additional information is necessary to assess risk posed by related organizations, the examiner should request that sufficient information be obtained during the examination to allow for an informed evaluation.

While GLBA limits the ability of an examiner to request information directly from functionally regulated entities, examiners may seek information about an FRE's risks from the bank's oversight and risk management system.

Types of Risk Posed by Related Organizations

It is difficult to generalize about the types of risks posed to a bank's safety and soundness by its related organizations. The amount of risk posed to the bank by any specific risk in a related organization depends on the nature of the organization's activities and its relationship to the bank. Routine business activities between a bank and its related organizations could subject the bank to any or all of the nine types of risk identified below. An operating subsidiary through which a bank conducts a significant line of business, such as a mortgage subsidiary, will pose much different risks from those of the local retail store that is owned by a community bank's controlling owner and transacts no business with the bank.

Reputation risk is common to almost all related organizations. When a bank's name is closely associated with another entity (even if the two do not transact business together), the bank may suffer loss of business or other harm if the related organization experiences financial difficulties or receives adverse publicity.

Strategic risk exists when a bank uses related entities to offer products and services to its customers without implementing appropriate oversight controls, or when those products and services are not compatible with the bank's strategic goals or customers' expectations.

Credit risk is posed to the bank when related organizations borrow from the bank, although this risk is limited by the quantitative and qualitative restrictions of sections 23A and 23B. However, credit risk can also arise when an affiliated third party fails to meet the terms of any contract with the bank or otherwise to perform as agreed.

Transaction risk is a function of internal controls, information systems, and operating processes. It is most evident in the case of an affiliated third party that is responsible for the bank's information and transaction processing or that provides products or services to the bank's customers.

The numerous laws and regulations that bar or limit extensions of credit to and other transactions with affiliates raise the possibility of substantial *compliance risk.*

Depending on the circumstances, relationships with affiliated entities may also subject the bank to *liquidity, interest rate, price,* and *foreign currency translation risk.*

Assessing the Different Types of Related Organizations

Holding Companies

The FRB is the primary supervisory authority over BHCs. However, the OCC has limited authority, pursuant to 12 USC 481, to examine BHCs and their nonbanking subsidiaries that are affiliated with national banks. Section 305 of the Riegle Community Development and Regulatory Improvement Act of 1994, 12 USC 1820(d), requires each federal banking agency, to the extent practical and consistent with principles of safety and soundness, to coordinate examinations of an insured depository institution with those of the institution's affiliates. Such examinations should be coordinated even if more than one federal agency is involved. The "Bank Supervision Process" booklet of the *Comptroller's Handbook* provides more detail on coordination between the regulators.

There are also situations in which certain special-purpose national banks are owned by holding companies that are not regulated by the FRB. The following guidance applies in those cases, as well.

Examiners should determine whether the holding company structure has strengthened the individual bank by providing financial support, diversification, economies of scale, and specialized management support, or has weakened the bank by introducing undue concentrations of credit, noncompliance with law or bank policy, and insufficient management talent.

Examiners will review transactions between the bank and the holding company, including extensions of credit and fees paid for services provided.

Examiners should consider the following factors when assessing the financial and operational effect of the parent company on the bank's operations: management, financial support, diversification and control, economies of scale, and taxes.

Management

A primary benefit of affiliation with a holding company is the availability of management expertise in many diverse areas. The holding company structure can help bank management considerably by providing expertise when specialized knowledge is essential. Management training programs within the holding company also provide the basis for successor management at the bank level.

However, the availability of and use of the parent holding company's directors and management at the bank may lead to conflicts of interest. Many of a parent company's directors and managers often serve in the same capacities at a subsidiary bank. One-bank holding companies sometimes have the same board and management as the bank. Similarly, a multibank holding company with centralized operations is often characterized by the placement of directors and officers of the parent company (or those of the lead bank) in each of its bank subsidiaries. In this scenario, the parent company or lead bank usually controls such activities as investment portfolio management, budgeting, tax planning, personnel management, correspondent banking, loan participations, and asset-liability management. While such structures can provide benefits, including necessary expertise and economies of scale, banks should guard against the possibility that persons who serve in dual capacities will have conflicts of interest.

Weaknesses in holding company management may leave the subsidiary bank without a consistent strategic direction, and can compromise the bank's risk management systems and inhibit the communication of risk tolerances. Conflicts of interest, poor administration, and other legal or control breaches may leave the bank vulnerable to changing market or regulatory conditions. If senior management maintains a dual role and tries to divide time between holding company and bank affairs, performance in both capacities may suffer.

The expansion and diversification of a holding company may cause subsidiary bank management to move to the holding company, leaving a void at the bank level. It is important, therefore, for the examiner to consider the impact of holding company management on the subsidiary bank.

Corporate policies should recognize the potential for conflicts of interest and provide guidance for resolution when cross-purposes exist. The overriding principle should be that the bank subsidiary should not be disadvantaged by a transaction with its parent company or any other affiliate.

Financial Support

A sound, well-managed bank holding company can be a source of strength for its subsidiary banks. However, if the parent company or its nonbank subsidiaries are not sound, the operation of the subsidiary banks can be adversely affected.

The "source of strength" doctrine is a fundamental and long-standing principle underlying the FRB's supervision and regulation of BHCs.[21] In return for pledging to support its subsidiary bank, a BHC is allowed to acquire an institution that can issue federally insured deposits. In serving as a source of strength for its subsidiary banks, a BHC should stand ready to use available resources to provide adequate capital funds to its subsidiary banks during periods of financial distress or adversity and should maintain the financial flexibility and capital-raising capacity to obtain additional resources for assisting its subsidiary banks. (See 12 CFR 225.4(a)(1).)

Consistent with the FRB's "source of strength" doctrine, a BHC structure can provide subsidiary banks with strong financial support because of the holding company's ability to shift funds to the bank, if needed, from other entities in the consolidated organization. The financial support can take the form of capital (equity or debt) or the funding of loans and investments. In general, the lower the BHC's leverage, the less likely the BHC will be to require cash flow from the banks to service its debt, and the more likely it will be to be able to serve as a source of financial strength to its bank subsidiaries.

---

[21] Section 2010.0 of the FRB's "Bank Holding Company Supervision Manual" discusses the "source of strength" principle.

When the financial condition of the parent company is tenuous, the parent may exert pressures on the subsidiary bank. To service its debt or provide support to other nonbank subsidiaries, the parent company may pressure a subsidiary bank to:

- Pay excessive dividends.

- Pay excessive management fees or other fees to affiliates.

- Purchase inadequate or unnecessary services from affiliates.

- Invest in high-risk assets to increase asset yields.

- Purchase the parent's or other affiliate's lower quality assets, or trade its high-quality assets for such assets.

- Make improper tax payments or unfavorably alter its tax situation.

Such activities are unsafe and unsound. The dividend policies of a national bank should be consistent with its capacity to pay and should not be based solely on the needs of shareholders or related organizations.

Debt service requirements of a holding company or other related organization may not be imposed upon or allocated to a national bank through management or other fees unless the fees represent reasonable reimbursement for goods and services that meet the legitimate needs of the bank. Generally, fees that are established solely to meet a shareholder or related organization's need for funds and that exceed the value of goods and services received will be cited as an unsafe and unsound banking practice. Such fees may also violate section 23B. Such activity dissipates profits and capital and disserves the financial interests of minority shareholders. Examiners should ensure that the fees being paid represent reasonable reimbursement for goods and services received.

Even when a holding company's structure is financially sound, the holding company's practice of selling long-term debt and passing the proceeds down to its bank subsidiary in the form of equity capital still may present problems. Although such a practice, frequently referred to as "double leveraging," increases the subsidiary bank's equity capital, the holding company must usually service its debts out of dividends from the subsidiary. If the subsidiary bank encounters an earnings problem, it may not be able to pay sufficient dividends to the holding company.

Another problem may develop when the holding company sells commercial paper and funds its subsidiary's loans with the proceeds. If the maturities of the commercial paper sold and the loans bought are not matched, and if the volume of such funding is large in relation to the subsidiary's overall operations, the practice may cause a liquidity problem.

A holding company may weaken a subsidiary bank by requiring it to maintain compensating balances to support holding company debt. In such a scenario, a holding company (or a nonbank subsidiary of a holding company) has a loan outstanding with a nonaffiliated bank. As a condition of granting the loan, the nonaffiliated bank requires the holding company's subsidiary bank to provide a compensating balance. Such a transaction should be cited as an unsafe and unsound banking practice when the holding company provides insufficient compensation to its subsidiary bank for the use of the funds. When the subsidiary bank receives adequate compensation, the transaction need not be criticized (unless the arrangement has other unfavorable aspects, such as a requirement that the bank place deposits in excess of what would normally support holding company borrowings).

Federal Reserve Inspection Reports will provide financial and operational information on the activities and soundness of the holding company.

Diversification and Control

To ensure orderly expansion and diversification, there must be adequate coordination among the banking and nonbanking subsidiaries within the parent holding company. Sound internal controls must be established to ensure that geographically dispersed or organizationally separated operations follow stated policies and procedures. The coordination of policies and internal controls are particularly important in the lending area. A major benefit to the individual bank in belonging to a multibank holding company is that it can better serve its customers by syndicating loans that would exceed its legal limit.

The ease with which loans are syndicated in a multibank holding company can, absent the proper policies and controls, expose the entire corporate

family to two hazards. The first relates to management: loans may be approved that are beyond the individual bank's lending limit and beyond the management expertise of any of the participants. The second relates to credit concentration: for multibank holding companies actively involved in the operations of affiliate banks, the absence of good communication may result in an undue concentration of credit. The problems of credit concentration are often magnified when nonbank affiliates, such as mortgage or leasing companies, are involved. A concentration of credit may develop when such nonbanking affiliates are extending credit to the same customers or industries as their affiliated banks.
\

Economies of Scale

The holding company structure can provide significant economies of scale in such areas as centralized information processing and risk management systems, such as internal audit. Despite the operating efficiencies that may be a result of centralized functions and processes, the bank should never relinquish total control of a bank function to the holding company. Such activities should be monitored closely and overseen by the bank's board of directors and management to ensure that the best interests of the bank are being properly protected. Examiners should review the functions and services that are outsourced to the holding company to ensure that controls are appropriate and that fees paid to the holding company are reasonable. OCC Bulletin 2001–47, "Third-Party Relationships," explains how a bank should oversee its relationship with its holding company and other related organizations that provide services for the bank or its customers.

Taxes

A holding company and its banking subsidiaries often will file a consolidated income tax return. However, each bank is viewed as, and reports as, a separate legal and accounting entity for regulatory purposes. Accordingly, the accrual of the current and deferred portions of each bank's applicable income taxes, reflecting either an expense or benefit, should be recorded as if the institution had filed as a separate entity. Furthermore, the amount and timing of payments or refunds should be no less favorable to the subsidiary than if it were a separate taxpayer. Any practice undertaken by a bank or holding company that is not consistent with this policy may be viewed as an unsafe and unsound practice prompting either informal or formal corrective action.

See the interagency policy statement "Income Tax Allocation in a Holding Company Structure" for additional information.

Subsidiaries

Except with respect to functionally regulated activities, national bank subsidiaries are normally supervised on a consolidated basis along with the parent bank.[22] For supervisory purposes, the bank and its operating subsidiaries are viewed as a single economic entity. The OCC ordinarily supervises national banks by business line, and, unless law or regulation provide otherwise, the terms and conditions that apply to national banks' activities are the same whether those activities are conducted directly or through an operating subsidiary. The results of operations of operating subsidiaries are consolidated with those of its parent for purposes of applying statutory or regulatory limits, such as lending limits or dividend restrictions.

Financial subsidiaries are treated differently. A national bank may not consolidate the assets and liabilities of a financial subsidiary with those of the bank. In addition, GLBA provides that other regulators will functionally regulate insurance and securities activities conducted by a financial subsidiary of a national bank. Consistent with GLBA, the OCC assesses the consolidated risk profile of a bank and its systems for monitoring and controlling the risks that are presented by its functionally regulated subsidiaries.

When an investment in a subsidiary is subject to the standard review process or when a bank requests an opinion, the OCC is able to perform both a legal and supervisory assessment of the proposal and may impose certain conditions of approval. However, if the activity is subject to only after-the-fact notice or if no notice or approval is required and the bank does not request an opinion, the OCC will not have an opportunity to evaluate and review the activity in advance for potential supervisory concerns.

In reviewing filings related to corporate activities, the examiner should ascertain that the OCC has issued final approval letters for the bank's newly established subsidiaries, unless the subsidiary qualified for after-the-fact notice or no notice under the regulation. If these approvals were subject to

---

[22] As discussed earlier, GLBA provides for the functional regulation of insurance and securities activities conducted by national bank subsidiaries and affiliates.

conditions, the examiner should assess whether bank management and the board of directors have addressed such conditions. If the bank filed an after-the-fact notice or did not file any notice, examiners should determine that the bank was eligible to use this procedure and that the activity the bank is engaged in also qualifies for this treatment.

If the bank's investment in the subsidiary is material or poses new or increased risks, the examiner should review the activities of the subsidiary to determine how the risk is managed and whether those activities are being conducted in a safe, sound, and legal manner. In determining the extent of this review, an examiner should consider:

- The subsidiary's line of business, and the nature of and inherent risk in that line of business.

- The extent to which the parent bank participates in that line of business, and the adequacy of the parent bank's policies, procedures, and risk management systems for that line of business.

- The percentage of ownership and the dollar amount invested in the subsidiary.

- The size of the subsidiary relative to the bank's total assets and capitalization.

- The types of services the subsidiary performs for the bank or other related organizations.

- The subsidiary's earnings contribution to the bank.

- The types and amounts of intercompany transactions, with a focus on compliance with sections 23A and 23B and Regulation W.

- The adequacy of the bank's policies and procedures governing subsidiaries.

If the investment in the subsidiary is material or poses new or increased risks to the bank, the examiner will refer to the sections of the *Comptroller's Handbook* that apply to the subsidiary's line of business for detailed guidance and examination procedures.

Chain Banking Organizations

OCC identifies and supervises banks that are part of a chain banking organization by assessing the condition of the banking group as a whole in addition to the safety and soundness of each national bank member. The lead national bank is usually the largest national bank (total assets as of the previous year-end) in the chain banking organization or the national bank in which management or shared functions are centralized. A lead national bank should be designated even if the actual lead bank is a state-chartered bank.

From a supervisory standpoint, chain banking organizations are very similar in character to multibank holding companies. Linking several banks or holding companies into a chain concentrates banking resources in a manner that may be vulnerable to common risks. Mutually shared risks that can arise in chain banking relationships may result from poor loan participation practices, common deficiencies in policies on such matters as lending and investments, domineering or absentee ownership, or insider abuses and other self-serving practices. Detection and correction of these problems largely depend upon an assessment of the entire chain banking organization that is often complicated when the chain is composed of institutions subject to different federal or state regulatory agencies. Additionally, unlike multibank holding companies, chain banking organizations do not have to report financial information on a consolidated basis, making supervisory monitoring more challenging.

The supervisory objectives of a chain banking organization review are to:

- Determine the financial condition of the consolidated group.

- Identify systemic risk issues by evaluating the effectiveness of the group's plans, policies, procedures, systems, and controls, if centralized.

- Evaluate the impact of the consolidated group on the condition and operations of the individual national banks.

- Determine compliance with laws governing transactions with affiliates.

The supervisory office of the lead national bank in a chain banking organization is responsible for developing a supervisory strategy for the chain banking organization in accordance with the supervisory cycle of the lead national bank (12 or 18 months). Such strategy should be risk-based and tailored to each chain banking organization on such factors as:

- The size, complexity, and sophistication of the chain bank organization, including how centralized its operations are.

- The managerial style and nature of control or influence being exerted over individual banks in the chain.

- The amount of interdependence among the individual institutions in the group. Particular attention should be paid to the volume and frequency of interbank transactions such as loan participations or sales, loans to insiders and their related interests, bank holding company or bank stock loans, correspondent or interbank transfers, contractual obligations for services, and purchases or sales of securities or other assets.

- The size, historical performance, nature and extent of problems, and overall condition of individual institutions in the group.

The supervisory office should determine the scope of the review in a manner that will effectively and efficiently carry out the supervisory objectives for chain banking organization reviews. Activities conducted may be part of specific on-site activities, periodic monitoring, or a combination of the two.

The supervisory office will coordinate, as appropriate, the examinations of national banks in the chain and the sharing of information with other OCC supervisory offices and regulatory agencies. When supervisory responsibility is shared with other regulatory agencies, examiners should coordinate with other regulators as discussed in the "Bank Supervision Process" booklet of the Comptroller's Handbook.

The supervisory office is responsible for documenting in Examiner View a summary analysis of the chain banking organization review as a "significant event" for the lead national bank of the chain. The summary analysis is intended to provide meaningful information about the chain banking group that is not provided in the reports of examination (ROE) on individual banks within the group. The analysis should identify any significant risks to the banks in the group and include a brief description of the financial condition of the consolidated group. The analysis also may address, as appropriate and consistent with the scope of the review, each CAMELS area, the audit and other risk management programs (if centralized), future plans and strategies, litigation, intercompany transactions, and necessary follow-up for the lead national bank and affiliated national banks.

The supervisory office also is responsible for maintaining in Examiner View core knowledge information documenting the chain bank relationship. These records contain the name of any individual (or group of individuals acting in concert) who owns or controls two or more banks or financial institutions in a chain banking organization. These records also may include information concerning the lead bank and each chain bank member, such as the name and location, charter number, supervisory agency, date of last chain bank review, date of next scheduled chain bank review, and the composite CAMELS ratings from the most recent examination.

Parallel-Owned Banking Organizations

Risks associated with parallel-owned banking groups arise from transactions with foreign affiliates that may be difficult to detect since the foreign affiliates do not receive direct U.S. supervisory oversight and the parallel-owned banking group's corporate structure limits comprehensive, consolidated home country supervision. Identifying and monitoring these risks often presents special supervisory challenges for the OCC.

The fundamental risk presented by these organizations is that they may be acting in a *de facto* organizational structure that, because it is not formalized, is not subject to comprehensive consolidated supervision. In addition, it may be difficult to obtain information from foreign supervisory agencies, and coordinated examinations of the U.S. bank and the parallel-owned foreign bank(s) may not be a viable option. Also, parallel banking groups in the United States are not subject to the "Foreign Bank Supervision Enhancement Act of 1991," which amended the International Bank Act of 1978, 12 USC 3101-3111. This act requires that foreign banking organizations seeking entry into the United States must be subject to comprehensive, consolidated supervision by their home country supervisors before they establish a banking presence in the United States.

The following examples are some of the primary reasons that supervisory risks arise from parallel-owned banking organizations:

- Officers and directors of the U.S. depository institution may be unable or unwilling to exercise independent control to ensure that transactions with the foreign parallel bank or affiliates are legitimate and comply with applicable laws and regulations.

- Money-laundering concerns may be heightened because transactions between the U.S. depository institution and the foreign parallel bank may not take place at arm's length.

- Securities, custodial, and trust transactions may be preferential to the extent that assets, earnings, and losses are artificially allocated among parallel banks. Similarly, low-quality assets and problem loans can be shifted among parallel banks to manipulate earnings or losses and avoid regulatory scrutiny.

- Political, legal, or economic events in the foreign country may affect the U.S. depository institution.

These and other risks are addressed more fully in the Joint Agency Statement on Parallel-Owned Banking Organizations, dated April 23, 2002.

When examiners identify a bank as part of a parallel banking relationship, the supervisory office is responsible for identifying in Examiner View the existence of the parallel banking relationship. If an institution is suspected of being a parallel bank, the examiner should contact International Banking & Finance (IB&F) to discuss the facts and circumstances surrounding the institution. IB&F, in consultation with the Law Department, will make the final determination as to whether a bank qualifies as a parallel bank under the guidelines. Likewise, any proposed modifications to existing parallel banking structures should be communicated to IB&F for their review and concurrence.

In developing the supervisory strategy for a U.S. national bank that is part of a parallel banking group, much consideration should be given to existing or possible risks arising from the lack of consolidated supervision for the parallel banking group, especially if the U.S. national bank is actively engaged in business activity with its foreign parallel bank. The examiner-in-charge of the U.S. parallel bank(s) will want to better understand the condition of the foreign parallel bank and be abreast of any supervisory concerns or developments in the home country. IB&F serves as the liaison with the foreign parallel bank's home country supervisor to facilitate exchanging necessary information about the parallel banking relationship. This exchange is an integral part of the examination process for active parallel banking groups. Additionally, the examiners may need IB&F's assistance in understanding political, legal, and economic developments in the foreign country that may affect the parallel U.S. bank. For example, events in the foreign country may trigger a rapid inflow or outflow of deposits at the U.S. bank, directly impacting its liquidity and risk perception, or reducing the foreign owner's ability to serve as a source of strength to the U.S. bank.

When supervisory responsibility is shared with other regulatory agencies, examiners should follow the guidance on examination coordination found in the "Bank Supervision Process" booklet of the *Comptroller's Handbook*. Whenever possible, the consolidated parallel banking group's U.S. operations should be reviewed concurrently.

Foreign Branches and Subsidiaries

On-site examinations of foreign branches and subsidiaries can be an important part of the supervisory program of a national bank. The need for on-site examination in a host country jurisdiction is driven by a number of factors, including the size of the branch or subsidiary operations, the types of activities in which the foreign branches and subsidiaries engage, the level of risk posed to the institution, and the ability off OCC examiners to obtain information and records directly from the parent bank. While on-site examinations sometimes may pose a problem because foreign directors, minority shareholders, or host country supervisors raise objections, many countries have eradicated previously identified barriers, such as secrecy provisions, that prevented on-site examinations. The international standard, as identified in the Basel Committee's 1996 paper, "The Supervision of Cross-border Banking," is that "host supervisors should, within the limits of their laws, be willing to cooperate with any home supervisor that wishes to make an inspection." In some cases, the host supervisor may impose conditions on the on-site examination work, such as requiring that the host be allowed to participate in the examination with the OCC. All conditions should be reviewed and considered prior to the start of the on-site work. Examiners should contact IB&F when issues arise concerning the ability to conduct an on-site examination in a jurisdiction or when assistance in coordinating with or informing the host supervisor on OCC plans to conduct an examination is required.

In those countries where it appears that secrecy laws, overly restrictive host country conditions, or other prohibitions could hinder on-site examination work in the host jurisdiction, there are other mechanisms that may be used to ensure that sufficient information is obtained about the branch or subsidiary. These mechanisms may include a Memorandum of Understanding or other informal information-sharing agreement, or direct negotiation of on-site work with the host supervisors. PPM 5500-1(rev), "Communications with Foreign Bank Supervisors," dated August 2002, provides more detail about sharing information with foreign supervisors.

In addition to these efforts, reports filed by foreign branches and subsidiaries under Regulation K or reports to foreign banking supervisors can provide a basis for evaluating the bank's investment. Regulation K requires that an effective system of records, controls, and reports be in place that keep the bank's management informed of the activities and condition of its foreign branches and subsidiaries. The FRB is required to examine Edge Act corporations annually and to produce a report of their examination. Examiners should review these reports as part of the examination of the parent bank.

Other Related Organizations

Examiners also will assess the risks posed by significant related organizations in which the bank has no direct investment. Such companies, often nonbanking subsidiaries of a bank holding company, may conduct activities as varied as lending, consumer leasing, data processing, broker-dealer operations, asset management, real estate appraisal, and property management for other real estate owned and bank premises. Affiliates often offer the bank an opportunity to engage in businesses otherwise prohibited for the bank. Yet because of the commonality of ownership or management, a bank's transactions with affiliates may not be subject to the same sort of objective analysis that transactions with independent parties receive. Even if the bank does not have a financial stake in the affiliate, any business setbacks of the affiliate may affect the condition of the bank. Therefore, assessing risks will require examiners to be knowledgeable about the businesses of all affiliates, the nature of affiliates' relationship with the bank, and all transactions between affiliates and the bank.

Like the risks posed by subsidiaries, the risks posed by affiliates depend on the nature of the affiliate's activities and its relationship to the bank. Even if a national bank does not transact business with an affiliate, the affiliate's business nevertheless may pose many indirect risks to the bank. For example, a full-scale mortgage affiliate may be subject to credit risk (obligor's repayment ability), interest rate risk (balance sheet repricing opportunities), transaction risk (the volume and complexity of transactions), liquidity risk (the volume, composition, and cost of funds), price risk (changes in value of position-taking instruments), compliance risk (adherence to consumer protection laws and other prescribed practices), reputation risk (the public's perception of the affiliate, particularly when the affiliate has the same trade name or brand as the bank), strategic risk (decisions affecting corporate mission and culture), and, conceivably, foreign currency translation risk (if the entity conducts transactions denominated in a foreign currency). A broker-dealer affiliate that sells nondeposit investment products to the bank's retail customers likely may be subject to transaction, compliance, strategic, and reputation risk. While these risks may not be unmitigated risks of the bank, the examiner should be aware of the types of risk associated with the affiliated entity in determining the level of risk posed to the bank.

For these related organizations, including related interests of insiders, examiners should focus on intercompany transactions. Intercompany transactions may pose other risks than simply compliance risk. Credit transactions with, or purchases of loans or other assets from, an affiliate also would directly subject the bank to credit risk, although the restrictions of sections 23A and 23B and Regulation W limit that risk. Intercompany transactions in the aggregate also may pose direct liquidity risk and interest rate risk. If there are few or no transactions between the bank and the affiliate, risk may be limited to reputation or strategic risk.

While affiliated enterprises often provide valuable support and expertise to a bank in areas such as information processing and property management, examiners should thoroughly review the fees paid to such affiliates to ensure that they are reasonable reimbursement for goods and services received and that they comply with section 23B.

Examination Procedures

General Procedures

Examiners should determine the effect of related organizations on the bank's safety and soundness by assessing the risks posed to the bank by the current and planned activities of the related organizations. The following procedures supplement the core assessment standards in the "Community Bank Supervision" and "Large Bank Supervision" booklets of the *Comptroller's Handbook*. Using the core assessment standards, examiners can assess risks for most legal entities and products. After considering the bank's risk profile and outstanding supervisory issues, examiners should perform appropriate additional procedures from the procedures below to determine the level of risk posed by its related organizations and the adequacy of the bank's risk management systems.

National banks and their operating subsidiaries are normally examined on a consolidated line of business basis without regard to corporate structure. Operating subsidiaries are subject to the same supervision and regulation as the parent bank, unless otherwise provided by law or regulation. In assessing the bank's risk profile, examiners will consider the risks posed by operating subsidiaries when developing an appropriate consolidated supervisory strategy for the bank and when performing supervisory activities.

When the activities, products, or lines of business in a bank, bank subsidiary, or other related organization warrant additional attention, examiners should perform appropriate expanded examination procedures from the booklet of the *Comptroller's Handbook* that applies to the particular activity. For example, the "Mortgage Banking" booklet should be used for an operating subsidiary conducting mortgage activities.

Regardless of the nature of business being conducted by a related organization, the bank should have policies, procedures, and internal controls that are specific to the relationship, both financial and operational, between the bank and the bank's related organizations.

In determining whether policies, procedures, and controls are adequate, examiners should consider, among other things, the results of internal audits, other internal compliance reviews, and external audits; the effectiveness of internal controls and management information systems; and work performed by other regulatory agencies. The following procedures will facilitate the assessment and should be used as appropriate in light of the risk posed to the bank by its related organizations.

Objective: Determine the scope of the examination of related organizations.

1. Obtain and review the following documents to identify any previous problems that require follow-up:

   - "Supervisory Strategy" and "Supervisory Concerns" in the OCC database.

   - EIC's scope memorandum.

   - Previous report of examination.

   - Internal and external audit reports and reports of other internal compliance review units.

   - Examination reports prepared by other regulators, if available.

2. Review the following information to determine if new related organizations exist:

   - Board minutes.

   - Bank-prepared listing of related organizations.

   - Bank financial statement and annual report.

   - Bank holding company reports.

   - Shareholder lists, officer and director statements of business interests/borrowing forms, and minutes to meetings of the board of directors.

   - FRB holding company inspection reports and state reports of bank holding company activities.

   - SEC reports, if applicable.

   - Examination reports of other regulatory agencies, including functional regulators, as available.

   - OCC's corporate activity information system.

- OCC's supervisory information system.

3. Discuss the bank's related organizations with bank management, legal staff, internal/external auditors, examiner liaison, and other staff members, as appropriate, to determine:

    - How management supervises and controls the risks associated with the bank's related organizations.

    - The line of business in which each related organization engages.

    - The relationship between the bank and each related organization.

    - How management responded to previously identified problems or concerns.

4. Obtain:

    - The bank's percentage of ownership and dollar amount invested in each related organization.

    - A list of transactions between the bank and each related organization, including loans to each entity, investments in it, and payments to or received from it. (High volume or recurring transactions may be grouped. For example, a monthly payment to a parent company for the performance of information technology services need be listed only once.)

    - A list of the services performed for or on behalf of the bank by each related organization, the services performed for or on behalf of each related organization by the bank, and the fees paid by or received from the bank for those services.

    - A list of assets, including market value, pledged as security for extensions of credit to each affiliate.

    - The types and amounts of assets involved in purchases, sales, or swaps between the bank and each related organization.

    - A list of the bank's contingent liabilities as a result of acts of any related organization, or as a result of litigation, claims, or assessments pending against a bank subsidiary or other related organization.

5. For operating subsidiaries and financial subsidiaries not previously reviewed, determine that the activity is being conducted as described in the bank's filing and as the OCC approved (as applicable).

6. If approval of an operating subsidiary was subject to conditions, determine whether bank management and the board of directors have abided by the conditions.

7. Provide information on each related organization to the examiner responsible for the examination of the line of business each related organization is engaged in.

8. Based on what was learned from these procedures, discussions with examiners responsible for the line of business each related organization is engaged in, and discussions with the bank EIC, determine the scope of this examination and its objectives.

9. Select from among the following examination procedures, as necessary, to determine the level of risk and the effectiveness of the risk management processes for the bank's related organizations.

10. If the scope of the review needs further expansion based on perceived risk, select from among the examination procedures in the booklet of the *Comptroller's Handbook* for the related organization's line of business.

Quantity of Risk

Conclusion: The quantity of risk is (low, moderate, high).

Objective: Determine the level of risk arising from relationships between the bank and its related organizations and whether those relationships pose undue risks upon the condition and reputation of the bank.

1. Review the list of related organizations and determine the type of related organization (for example: nonbank affiliate, operating subsidiary, financial subsidiary, statutory subsidiary, bank holding company, chain banking organization, parallel banking group, community development investment, foreign branch).

2. Identify the lines of business in which each related organization engages.

3. Through review of bank-prepared information and discussions with bank personnel, identify the nature of the relationship or manner of affiliation between the bank and its related organizations. Determine which related organizations are affiliates for purposes of applying the legal restrictions on transactions with affiliates.

4. Assess whether the bank maintains sufficient independence in its relationships with its parent company and other related organizations to ensure that the interests of the bank are adequately protected and not subordinate to those of the related organization.[23] Consider:

   • Does the bank have an appropriate conflicts of interest policy and is compliance with the policy monitored?

   • If the board and management of the bank are the same or predominantly the same as that of the parent company or other material related organization, is there guidance for resolving any conflicts of interest presented by these dual roles?

   • Does bank policy provide for transparency of reporting of affiliate transactions and require that those transactions be subject to internal and external audit?

---

[23] National bank operating subsidiaries are not viewed as independent organizations since their results of operations are consolidated with the parent bank. National banks and their operating subsidiaries are examined on a consolidated line of business basis without regard to corporate form.

- Are dealings with related organizations subject to appropriate oversight by the bank's board and management, including risk management systems and management information systems (MIS)?

- Do related organizations provide significant services to the bank or perform significant functions for the bank and, if so, is payment for those services reasonable and well-documented?

- Is the formation of or investment in new related organizations, or the introduction of new or complex activities within existing related organizations, subject to adequate due diligence by the bank?

- Do board or committee meeting minutes reflect discussions of material related organizations and reflect approval of significant dealings or transactions?

5. Assess the financial condition and quality of operations of the related organization, as appropriate.

6. Identify and determine the significance of any material changes in the bank's relationship with, investment in, or transactions with a related organization.

7. Determine the significance of any changes in the type or volume of the products that related organizations offer, or the significance of any changes in the vehicle through which related organizations offer those products.

8. Determine whether transactions between the bank and its related organizations are appropriate. Consider the following:

- When the transaction represents fees paid or received for services rendered,

  - The necessity of the service.

  - The quality of the service received.

  - The method used to compute the charge for the service.

  - The reasonableness of the costs incurred.

  - How the fee schedule compares with that in effect 12 months ago.

  - The bank's ability to afford such cost.

- Cash transfers to or from a related organization in connection with a consolidated income tax obligation (amounts paid should be based on the amount that would be due if a separate return were filed and should be paid only at such time to reasonably permit required estimated payments or final settlements to be made to the IRS).

- The quality and nature of loans, investments, or future commitments.

9. Review transactions between the bank and its affiliates. Consider:
   - The business function of each affiliate.

   - The nature of the relationship with the bank.

   - Risks applicable to each affiliate.

   - Risks that may translate directly to the bank.

   - Compliance with sections 23A and 23B and Regulation W.

10. Consider the following when determining the type and level of risk presented to the bank by *operating subsidiaries, financial subsidiaries,* and *statutory subsidiaries*:

    - Review information on the activities of each subsidiary and determine the materiality of the bank's investment in the subsidiary. Consider the following:

      - The percent of ownership and the dollar amount invested in the subsidiary.

      - The nature of risk and the level of risk inherent in the subsidiary's business.

      - The adequacy of the bank's policies and procedures governing the subsidiary's line of business.

      - The extent to which the parent bank participates in the subsidiary's line of business outside the subsidiary.

      - The size of the subsidiary relative to the bank's total assets and capitalization.

      - The types of services the subsidiary performs for the bank or other related organizations.

      - The subsidiary's contribution to the bank's earnings.

- The types and amounts of intercompany transactions.

- Determine which, if any, additional procedures from applicable booklets of the *Comptroller's Handbook* should be incorporated into the review.

11. Consider the following when determining the type and level of risk presented to the bank by a *bank holding company*:

- Review the management structure and programs of the holding company and its subsidiaries and consider the following:

  - The level of centralized control over the subsidiary bank.

  - Management expertise available to the subsidiary bank.

  - Management training programs.

  - Directors and senior managers who hold positions in the holding company and the subsidiary bank.

  - Bank management time allocated to holding company rather than bank business.

  - Conflicts of interest.

- Review and analyze holding company financial information and consider the following:

  - Bank payment of excessive dividends to the holding company.

  - Bank payment of excessive management or other fees.

  - Bank purchase of inadequate or unnecessary services from the holding company or other subsidiaries.

  - Holding company borrowings used to provide equity contributions to the subsidiary bank (double leverage).

  - Sale of commercial paper by the holding company to fund its bank subsidiary's loans.

  - Deposit relationships at the bank.

  - Income tax payments when a consolidated tax return is filed.

  - Transfer of assets between the holding company or other affiliates and the subsidiary bank.

12. Consider the following when determining the type and level of risk presented to the bank by *chain banking organizations*:

- Review OCC reports of examination, as well as those of other federal or state supervisors, on banks within a chain banking group for mutually shared risks. Consider the following:
    - Size and complexity of the organization.
    - Historical performance and overall condition of the institutions in the chain.
    - Financial condition of the consolidated group.
    - Degree and nature of control or influence over individual banks in the chain.
    - Degree of centralization of operations.
    - Degree of interdependence among the individual institutions in the group.
    - Effectiveness of centralized plans, policies, procedures, systems, and controls.
    - The volume and frequency of interbank transactions such as loan participations, loans to insiders and related interests, bank stock loans, interbank transfers, contractual obligations for services, and purchase or sale of assets.

13. Consider the following when determining the type and level of risk presented to the bank by *community development investments*:

- Determine whether the investment between the bank and its related community and economic development entity (CEDE) is consistent with 12 CFR 24's public welfare requirement. Consider:
    - Whether the bank's file or documentation indicates that the CEDE or CD project is consistent with the public welfare requirement of 12 CFR 24.3 or is a "qualified investment" under the Community Reinvestment Act.
    - Whether the public welfare activities provided or supported by the CEDE or CD project generally are consistent with the activities

acknowledged or approved by the OCC in response to the bank's after-the-fact notice or prior approval request.

- Determine whether the bank's investment in the CEDE or CD project is consistent with the investment limits of 12 CFR 24. Consider the following:

  - Whether the dollar amount of the bank's investment in the CEDE or CD project is consistent with the amount acknowledged or approved by the OCC in response to the bank's after-the-fact notice or prior approval request.

  - Whether the nature, type, or legal structure of the bank's investment in the CEDE or CD project is consistent with the OCC's acknowledgment or approval in response to the bank's after-the-fact notice or prior approval request.

  - Whether the investment exposes the bank to unlimited liability or results in noncompliance with 12 CFR 24's general prohibition of investment in OREO (unless the OCC has specifically permitted such investment).

- Determine whether the dollar amount of the bank's aggregate outstanding investments and commitments is within the investment limits of 12 CFR 24.4. Consider:

  - Whether the aggregate amount of the bank's investments under 12 CFR 24 is less than 5 percent of capital and surplus.

  - If the aggregate amount of the bank's investments under 12 CFR 24 is greater than 5 percent of capital and surplus, whether the OCC has permitted, in writing, an amount greater than the 5 percent limit (but in no event greater than 10 percent of capital and surplus).

  - Whether the bank uses generally accepted accounting procedures (GAAP) for calculating the aggregate amount of its community development investments. If the bank has used procedures other than GAAP, whether the OCC has, in writing, permitted use of such procedures.

  - The bank's system for tracking its community development investments and commitments, including investments that have been changed, completed, sold, or otherwise disposed of.

- Determine the effectiveness of the bank's process for notifying the OCC of its 12 CFR 24 investments. Consider:

  - Whether the bank used the appropriate process and form CD-1 for notifying the OCC about its investment in a CEDE or CD project.

  - The timeliness of the bank's form CD-1 submissions to the OCC.

  - Whether the bank notified the OCC about any changes in the amount or nature of its investment in the CEDE or CD project.

- Determine whether the bank maintains the appropriate information concerning its 12 CFR 24 investments. Consider:

  - Whether the bank's file or documentation for each investment is readily accessible and available for examination and supports the certifications contained in the after-the fact notice or investment proposal.

  - Whether the bank's file or documentation contains the OCC response to the after-the-fact notice or investment proposal for each investment.

  - If the OCC imposed one or more conditions in connection with its approval of an investment under 12 CFR 24, whether the bank's file or documentation indicates how the bank has complied with those conditions.

14. Consider the following when determining the type and level of risk presented to the bank by *international banking facilities*:
    - Determine that all deposits and extensions of credit by the IBF are only to qualified customers.

    - Determine that deposits and extensions of credit to foreign residents and foreign affiliates of U.S. corporations:

    - Are used only to support operations outside the United States, and

    - Meet the written notification and acknowledgement requirements.

    - Determine that IBF accounts are clearly segregated from the establishing entity's books.

    - Determine that IBF accounts meet the maturity or required notice period for withdrawal.

- Determine that deposits and withdrawals meet the minimum size transaction amount.

- Determine that IBF purchases of assets from third parties and sales of assets to third parties meet the eligible assets requirement, are transacted at arm's length without recourse, and meet the restrictions concerning transactions with U.S. affiliates.

15. Consider the following when determining the type and level of risk presented to the bank by *parallel-owned banking groups:*

    - Review OCC reports of examination, as well as those of other federal, state, or foreign supervisors. Consider the following:

        - The quantity and quality of information available from foreign bank supervisors.

        - The volume and frequency of transfers of assets between parallel banks.

        - The quality of supervision of the parallel banks.

        - The quality of assets transferred among the parallel banks.

        - The use of international stock purchase loans.

        - Concentrations of risk.

        - The impact of political, legal, and economic events in the foreign country.

16. Determine the propriety of the carrying value of the bank's investment in each related organization (including any loans made to it):

    - Evaluate the balance sheet and operating statement of the entity in which the bank has made the investment.

    - Review the quality of assets held by the entity, relating any classified assets to the capital structure of the company.

    - Based upon the above, determine the quality of the bank's investment in, and loans to, that company.

17. For each related organization that is a defendant in a lawsuit, determine whether the pending litigation could have an adverse effect on the bank.

Objective: Determine the level of compliance with the following applicable laws, rulings, and regulations:

Section 23A/12 USC 371c and Regulation W, Transactions with Affiliates

1. Determine which affiliates are exempt from these statutory requirements.

2. For each affiliate to which this statute applies, determine whether the aggregate amount of covered transactions with the bank and its subsidiaries exceeds 10 percent of capital and surplus.

3. For all affiliates to which this statute applies, determine whether the aggregate amount of covered transactions with the bank and its subsidiaries exceeds 20 percent of capital and surplus.

4. Determine whether extensions of credit to affiliates are secured by collateral with required market value.

5. Determine whether there have been impermissible transfers of low-quality assets to the bank from any of its affiliates.

6. Determine whether all transactions with affiliates are on terms and conditions that are consistent with safe and sound banking practices.

Section 23B/12 USC 371c–1 and Regulation W, Transactions with Affiliates

For affiliates to which this statute applies, determine that all transactions with affiliates are on terms and under conditions that are substantially the same, or at least as favorable to the bank or its subsidiary, as those prevailing at the time for comparable transactions with nonaffiliated companies (arm's length).

12 CFR 5.34, Operating Subsidiaries[24]

1. Determine whether the bank owns more than 50 percent of the outstanding voting stock in a corporation.

2. For new operating subsidiaries, new activities in an existing subsidiary, new noncontrolling investments through an operating subsidiary, or new investments in a bank service company, determine whether the appropriate corporate filings were submitted to the OCC.

12 CFR 5.39, Financial Subsidiaries[24]

1. Determine whether the bank qualifies for investing in a financial subsidiary and submitted the appropriate corporate notice and certifications.

2. Determine whether the bank meets the safety and soundness safeguards for engaging in activities through a financial subsidiary.

12 CFR 24, Community Development Investments

1. Determine whether the bank submitted the appropriate after-the-fact notice or investment proposal filings to the OCC.

2. Calculate the bank's aggregate outstanding investments and commitments as a percentage of capital and surplus and determine that the aggregate outstanding does not exceed 5 percent of capital and surplus, and with OCC approval, the aggregate does not exceed 10 percent of capital and surplus.

---

[24] These procedures for operating subsidiaries and financial subsidiaries pertain to licensing requirements only. National bank operating subsidiaries are subject to all of the laws and regulations applicable to the parent national bank, unless otherwise provided by law. Statutory limits, such as lending limits and dividend restrictions, are applied based on the consolidated results of the parent bank and its operating subsidiaries. Operating subsidiaries are integrated into the supervisory strategy of the parent national bank. Examiners will use appropriate procedures out of the booklets in the *Comptroller's Handbook* that pertain to the operating subsidiary's line of business.

3. Verify that the investments do not expose the bank to unlimited liability.

12 USC 618, Edge Act and Agreement Corporations

1. Calculate the bank's aggregate outstanding investment as a percentage of the bank's capital and surplus and determine that the aggregate outstanding does not exceed 10 percent of capital and surplus, and, in any case, and with FRB approval, the aggregate does not exceed 20 percent of capital and surplus.

Other Applicable Laws, Rulings, and Regulations

1. Review the list of the bank's related organizations and determine which other laws, rulings, and regulations apply. See the "References" section of this booklet for a detailed listing.

2. Determine whether the bank complies with these other laws, rulings, and regulations, as applicable.

Quality of Risk Management

Conclusion: The quality of risk management is (strong, satisfactory, weak)

Policy

Conclusion: The board (has, has not) established adequate policies governing related organizations.

Objective: Determine the adequacy of written policies relative to related organizations.

1. Review the bank's policies for related organizations and consider whether the policies:

    - Have been adopted by the board of directors and are periodically reviewed and updated.

    - Establish adequate guidelines and controls on:

        – The formation or acquisition of related organizations (due diligence). These policies are especially important when a related organization offers new or expanded services.

        – Dealings with related organizations, to ensure that they are carried out at arm's length and in the bank's best interests.

        – Transactions with affiliates and lending to insiders' related interests.

        – Bank functions and services, including risk management systems that are centralized in the holding company or performed by an affiliate on behalf of the bank.

        – Obtaining and maintaining adequate records and information, including independent audit reports. Such information should document the nature and financial status of significant related organizations.

        – Actual and potential conflicts of interest, to ensure that they are disclosed.

- Confidential customer information, to ensure that it remains confidential.

- Employee sharing, to ensure that such arrangements are not confusing for bank customers and do not harm the bank.

- Concentrations of credit, if the bank and any related organization(s) lend to the same customers or industries.

- Tying the availability of products or services offered by the bank to obtaining products or services offered by affiliates.

- Require the board to objectively review and monitor the performance of bank services or functions by its related organizations on behalf of the bank.

- Require the board to objectively review and monitor transactions between the bank and its related organizations.

- Require that transactions between the bank and its related organizations be subject to an independent audit.

- Address compliance with applicable laws, regulations, and rulings.

Processes

Conclusion: Management and the board (have, have not) implemented adequate policies and procedures to manage the risks associated with the bank's related organizations.

Objective: Determine the adequacy of policies and procedures in place to manage the relationship between the bank and its related organizations.

1. Obtain and review the operating policy guidelines and procedures relating to the bank's related organizations, paying particular attention to any changes since the previous examination.

2. Determine whether bank management and employees are operating in conformance with policy guidelines and procedures.

3. Determine whether the bank maintains current records on the form and status of each related organization.

4.   Review deficiencies noted during any internal or external audit or other bank reviews and determine why the deficiencies occurred.

5.   Review management response to deficiencies, actions implemented to address deficiencies, follow-up to test effectiveness of corrective actions, and plans to avoid deficiencies going forward.

Personnel

Conclusion: Bank management and personnel (are/are not) aware of the risks applicable to specific related organizations and related risk management activities.

Objective: Given the size and complexity of the bank's related organizations, determine whether bank management and personnel possess the skills and knowledge to understand and manage the risks arising from the bank's related organizations.

1. Obtain the following:

   • Résumés of bank management and personnel involved with related organizations.

   • Job descriptions of management and personnel in related organizations.

2. Discuss with appropriate bank management and personnel their roles and responsibilities regarding specific related organizations.

3. Assess management and personnel education, training, and experience in the line of business of the bank's related organizations. Consider:

   • Education and work experience.

   • Understanding of the laws, rulings, and regulations relative to related organizations.

   • Understanding of the risks inherent in the bank's related organizations and how the risks are being managed.

   • Expertise to effectively manage and oversee relationships in which bank functions, including risk management systems, are centralized at the holding company level or are performed by any other related organization.

   • Expertise to effectively manage loan participations and other transactions between the bank and its related organizations.

Controls

Conclusion: The board and management (have/have not) established an effective control system for related organizations.

Objective: Determine whether the board and senior management have established appropriate control systems for related organizations.

1. Review bank records, determine whether they are current, and record the following information about the form and status of each related organization:

    - Name.

    - Location.

    - Nature of business.

    - Manner of affiliation.

    - Relationship with the bank, including any bank functions or services that are performed on behalf of the bank.

    - Fees schedule for functions or services that are performed on behalf of the bank.

    - Amount of loans to, investments in, and other extensions of credit to the related organization.

    - Collateral pledged to secure any extension of credit to the related organization.

    - The organization's obligations that serve as collateral for advances made to others.

    - Commitments.

    - Litigation.

    - Any other pertinent information.

2. Assess the scope and adequacy of the internal and external audits of related organizations and management's response to those audits.

3.   Determine whether bank management and the board of directors properly monitor the activities of related organizations by considering whether they:

• Have developed policies and procedures governing the performance of bank functions or services by related organizations on behalf of the bank.

• Are an integral part of the related organization's management or board of directors.

• Have an active role in the related organizations' audit committees or retain the right to examine the organization's records (and to receive letters from the external auditors).

• Review and maintain a copy of all internal or external audit reports of its related organizations, including management letters and responses.

• Conduct periodic independent reviews to assess bank management objectives and policies with regard to the current status of their association with the related organizations.

4.   Assess the impact on bank operations of any senior manager who maintains roles in both the bank and the related organization, especially a role in a holding company.

5.   Review management information reports to determine whether they:

• Inform management and the board of directors about the activities and condition of the bank's related organizations.

• Identify and inform senior management about potential and actual concentrations of credit that are created when the bank and its nonbank affiliates lend to the same industry, customer, or type of customer.

• Identify and address the appropriateness of all transactions between affiliates.

6.   For all noncontrolling equity investments, determine whether the OCC has issued an opinion regarding permissibility. If an opinion letter has

not been issued, ensure that the following four standards have been satisfied:

- The activities of the entity in which the investment is made are limited to activities that are part of, or incidental to, the business of banking, or otherwise authorized for a national bank.

- The bank is able to prevent the enterprise from engaging in activities that do not meet the foregoing standard or is able to withdraw its investment.

- The investment must be useful to the bank in carrying out the bank's business rather than a passive investment unrelated to its banking business.

- The bank's loss exposure must be limited; i.e., the bank must not have open-ended liability for the obligations of the enterprise.

7. Determine whether the bank reviews and maintains copies of appropriate examination reports prepared by other functional regulators.

8. Determine whether records are maintained for the companies in which the bank has a capital investment, including foreign ones, indicating the extent of bank control, quality of assets, profitability of the company, and the legality of operations.

9. Review bank policies and determine, when the bank and a related organization conduct similar lines of business (for example, when the bank conducts mortgage lending activities and has a mortgage lending subsidiary), whether the activities are subject to a common set of controls.

10. Determine whether the bank has systems and controls to provide adequate training of employees and to promote compliance with anti-tying provisions.

11. Determine whether ownership interests in related organizations are accounted for in accordance with call report instructions.

12. To assess the adequacy of controls for a specific related organization, refer to the "Examination Procedures" section of the appropriate

booklet of the *Comptroller's Handbook* for the line of business of the related organization.

Conclusions

1.   Prepare written conclusion summaries, discuss findings with the EIC, and communicate findings to management. Areas to be covered should include:

   - The adequacy of the bank's policies, procedures, and controls.

   - The manner in which bank personnel operate in conformance with established policies.

   - The level of oversight provided by the board and management for related organizations that provide services and functions on behalf of the bank.

   - The adequacy of information on related organizations available for management and the board of directors.

   - Internal or external audit findings not acted upon by management, as well as any other concerns or recommendations resulting from review of the bank's related organizations.

   - Violations of laws, rulings, and regulations.

   - The quantity of risk and the quality of risk management for related organizations in general and each specific type of related organization reviewed.

   - Recommended corrective actions, if applicable, and management's commitments for corrective action.

2.   Determine how any applicable risk identified will affect aggregate risk and direction of risk. Examiners should refer to guidance provided under the OCC's large and community bank risk assessment programs.

3.   Determine, in consultation with the EIC, whether further review or examination of a type of related organization (or a specific related organization) is warranted.

   If so, discuss findings with the appropriate examiner and refer to the section of the *Comptroller's Handbook* that covers the line of business of the related organization for additional examination guidance.

If the related organization in question is a functionally regulated entity, the examiner must consult with the appropriate deputy comptroller before proceeding.

4. Determine, in consultation with the EIC, whether the risks identified are significant enough to merit bringing them to the board's attention in the report of examination.

    If so, prepare items for inclusion under the heading "Matters Requiring Attention."

5. Hold a meeting with appropriate bank oversight committees or the appropriate risk managers to communicate conclusions and recommendations, if appropriate and authorized by the bank EIC. Allow management sufficient time before the meeting to review the draft conclusions.

6. As appropriate, prepare a comment on related organizations for inclusion in the report of examination. The comment should discuss:

    - Adequacy of policies, procedures, personnel, and controls.

    - Significant problems disclosed by auditors that have not been corrected.

    - Any deficiencies or concerns reviewed with management, any corrective actions recommended by examiners, and management commitments for corrective actions.

7. Prepare a memorandum and update work programs with any information that will facilitate future examinations.

8. Update the OCC information database, which may include:

    - Matters Requiring Attention.

    - Risk Assessment System.

    - Violations of law or regulation.

    - Core knowledge database.

9.   Organize and reference work papers in accordance with OCC guidelines.

Appendix A

Operating Subsidiary Activities Qualifying for After-the-fact Notice

The activities qualifying for the after-the-fact notice process for operating subsidiaries are listed below:

- Holding and managing assets acquired by the parent bank, including investment assets and property acquired by the bank through foreclosure or otherwise in good faith to compromise a doubtful claim, or in the ordinary course of collecting a debt previously contracted.

- Providing services to or for the bank or its affiliates, including accounting, auditing, appraising, advertising and public relations, and financial advice and consulting.

- Making loans or other extensions of credit and selling money orders, savings bonds, and travelers checks.

- Purchasing, selling, servicing, or warehousing loans or other extensions of credit, or interests therein.

- Providing courier services between financial institutions.

- Providing management consulting, operational advice, and services for other financial institutions.

- Providing check guaranty, verification, and payment services.

- Providing data processing, data warehousing and data transmission products, services, and related activities and facilities, including associated equipment and technology for the bank or its affiliates.

- Acting as investment adviser (including an adviser with investment discretion) or financial adviser or counselor to governmental entities or instrumentalities, businesses, or individuals, including advising registered investment companies and mortgage or real estate investment trusts, furnishing economic forecasts or other economic information, providing investment advice related to futures and options on futures, and providing consumer financial counseling.

- Providing tax planning and preparation services.

- Providing financial and transactional advice and assistance, including advice and assistance for customers in structuring, arranging, and executing mergers and acquisitions, divestitures, joint ventures, leveraged buyouts, swaps, foreign exchange, derivative transactions, coin and bullion, and capital restructurings.

- Underwriting credit related insurance to the extent permitted under section 302 of GLBA (15 USC 6712).

- Leasing of personal property and acting as an agent or adviser in leases for others.

- Providing securities brokerage or acting as a futures commission merchant and providing related credit and other related services.

- Underwriting and dealing, including making a market, in bank permissible securities and purchasing and selling, as principal, asset-backed obligations.

- Acting as an insurance agent or broker, including title insurance to the extent permitted under section 303 of GLBA (15 USC 6713).

- Reinsuring mortgage insurance on loans originated, purchased, or serviced by the bank, its subsidiaries, or its affiliates, provided that if the subsidiary enters into a quota share agreement, the subsidiary assumes less than 50 percent of the aggregate insured risk covered by the quota share agreement. A "quota share agreement" is an agreement under which the reinsurer is liable to the primary insurance underwriter for an agreed upon percentage of every claim arising out of the covered book of business ceded by the primary insurance underwriter to the reinsurer.

- Acting as a finder pursuant to 12 CFR 7.1002 to the extent permitted by published OCC precedent.

- Offering correspondent services to the extent permitted by published OCC precedent.

- Acting as agent or broker in the sale of fixed or variable annuities.

- Offering debt cancellation or debt suspension agreements.

- Providing real estate settlement, closing, escrow, and related services; and real estate appraisal services for the subsidiary, parent bank, or other financial institutions.

- Acting as a transfer or fiscal agent.

- Acting as a digital certification authority to the extent permitted by published OCC precedent, subject to the terms and conditions contained in that precedent.

- Providing or selling public transportation tickets, event and attraction tickets, gift certificates, prepaid phone cards, promotional and advertising material, postage stamps, and Electronic Benefits Transfer (EBT) script, and similar media, to the extent permitted by published OCC precedent, subject to the terms and conditions contained in that precedent.

Appendix B

Primary Supervisory Banking Authority*	
OCC	National banks, operating subsidiaries of national banks (12 CFR 5.34), financial subsidiaries of national banks (12 CFR 5.39), statutory subsidiaries of national banks (12 USC 24), bank service companies**, foreign branches of national banks.
FRB	Parent bank holding companies, nonbank subsidiaries of bank holding companies, consolidated bank holding companies, state member banks, bank service companies**, Edge Act and Agreement Corporations.***
Federal Deposit Insurance Corporation	State nonmember banks, their operating subsidiaries, and their bank service companies.**
Office of Thrift Supervision	Federal savings associations, federal savings banks, state savings association (collectively, thrifts); operating subsidiaries, finance subsidiaries, and service corporations of thrifts; thrift holding companies, thrift holding company affiliates.
SEC	Brokerage activities of national banks, brokerage subsidiaries and affiliates of national banks.
State Insurance Commissioners	Insurance activities of national banks, insurance subsidiaries and affiliates of national banks.
Commodities Futures Trading Commission	Commodity futures and options activities of national banks, and affiliates of national banks engaged in such activities.

* GLBA imposes specific restrictions upon the OCC and other federal banking regulators concerning the examination of and requests for information from functionally regulated affiliates and subsidiaries.

** Bank service companies are subject to examination and regulation by the appropriate federal banking agency of its principal investor.

*** OCC has the authority to examine Edge Act and Agreement Corporations that are affiliates of national banks.

References

Accounting
Issuance	"General Instructions to the Consolidated Reports of Condition and Income"
Issuance	OCC 98–56, Interagency Policy Statement, "Income Tax Allocation in a Holding Company Structure"

Affiliate Transactions
Laws	12 USC 221a, 371c, 371c–1
Regulation	12 CFR 223

Agreement Corporation
Law	12 USC 603
Regulations	12 CFR 28.11, 211

Agricultural Credit Corporations
Law	12 USC 24(Seventh)

Annuities
Law	12 USC 24(Seventh)
Advisory Letter	AL 968

Banker's Bank
Law	12 USC 24(Seventh)

Bank Holding Company
Law	12 USC 1841
Regulation	12 CFR 225
Issuance	OCC 98–56, Interagency Policy Statement, "Income Tax Allocation in a Holding Company Structure"

Bank Ownership of Property
Law	12 USC 29
Regulation	12 CFR 7.1000

Bank Premises Corporation
Law	12 USC 371d
Regulations	12 CFR 5.37 and 7.1000
Issuance	*Comptroller's Licensing Manual,* "Investment in Bank Premises"

Bank Service Company
Laws	12 USC 1861–1867
	12 USC 1843(c)(8)
Regulation	12 CFR 5.35, 12 CFR 225.28
Bulletin	OCC 2001–47, "Third-Party Relationships"

Board and Management Responsibilities
Issuance	*The Director's Book,* OCC, March 1997
	"Red Flags in Board Reports—A Guideline for Directors," October 2003

Capital
Laws	12 USC 56 and 60, 1831o, 3907
Regulations	12 CFR 3 and 6

Chain Banking Organization
Regulation	12 CFR 5.50

Community Development Investments
Law	12 USC 24(Eleventh)
Regulation	12 CFR 24

Data Processing
Law	12 USC 24(Seventh)
Regulation	12 CFR 7.5002

Edge Act Corporation
Law	12 USC 611
Regulation	12 CFR 28.2, 28.11

Examination Authority
Laws	12 USC 481, 602

Federal Deposit Insurance Act

Law	12 USC 1811–1835a

Financial Subsidiary

Law	12 USC 24a
Regulation	12 CFR 5.39
Issuance	*Comptroller's Licensing Manual,* "Investments in Subsidiaries and Equities"

Functional Regulation

Law	12 USC 1831v
Regulation	12 CFR 5.39

Insider Activities

Laws	12 USC 375, 375a, and 375b
Regulations	12 CFR 31, 215
Issuance	*Comptroller's Handbook,* "Insider Activities"

Internal Controls

Issuance	*Comptroller's Handbook,* "Internal Control"

International Banking Activities

Law	12 USC 601–633
Regulation	12 CFR 28

International Banking Facility

Regulation	12 CFR 28.11

Leasing

Law	12 USC 24(Seventh), 24(Tenth)
Regulation	12 CFR 23

Limited Liability Company

Laws	12 USC 24(Seventh)
	12 USC 1861(a)(7)
Regulation	12 CFR 5.36

Operating Subsidiary
      Law   12 USC 24(Seventh)
      Regulation   12 CFR 5.34
      Issuance   *Comptroller's Licensing Manual*, "Investment in Subsidiaries and Equities"

Other Equity Investments
      Law   12 USC 24(Seventh)
      Regulation   12 CFR 5.36

Parallel-Owned Banking Organizations
      Regulation   12 CFR 5.50
      Issuance   OCC 2002–14, "Joint Agency Statement on Parallel-Owned Banking Organizations"

Prompt Corrective Action
      Law   12 USC 1831o
      Regulation   12 CFR 6

Regulation K
      Regulation   12 CFR 211

Regulation W
      Regulation   12 CFR 223

Safe Deposit Corporation
      Law   12 USC 24(Seventh)

Small Business Investment Company
      Law   15 USC 682(b)
      Regulation   12 CFR 7.1015

State Savings Association
      Law   12 USC 1813(b)(3)

Supervision Policy

Issuances
Comptroller's Handbook, "Bank Supervision Process"
Comptroller's Handbook, "Community Bank Supervision"
Comptroller's Handbook, "Examination Planning and Control"
Comptroller's Handbook, "Large Bank Supervision"
Comptroller's Handbook, "New Activities"
Comptroller's Handbook, "Insurance Activities"

Tying

Law
12 USC 1972

Regulation
12 CFR 225.7

Issuances
OCC 95–20, "Tying Restrictions"
Today's Credit Markets, Relationship Banking, and Tying (OCC September 2003)
Anti-Tying Restrictions of Section 106 of the Bank Holding Company Act Amendments of 1970 (FRB)

www.ingramcontent.com/pod-product-compliance
Lightning Source LLC
Chambersburg PA
CBHW052002280526
45793CB00005B/822